Christmas is Coming!

Vol. 6

Compiled and Edited
by Catherine Corbett Fowler

Oxmoor House®

page 132

©1996 by Oxmoor House, Inc.
Book Division of Southern Progress Corporation
P.O. Box 2463, Birmingham, Alabama 35201

Published by Oxmoor House, Inc., and Leisure Arts, Inc.

All rights reserved. No part of this book may be reproduced in any form or by any means without the prior written permission of the publisher, excepting brief quotations in connection with reviews written specifically for inclusion in magazines or newspapers, or single copies for strictly personal use.

Library of Congress Catalog Card Number: 94-65475
ISBN: 0-8487-1501-2
ISSN: 1074-8954
Manufactured in the United States
     of America
First Printing 1996

Editor-in-Chief: Nancy Fitzpatrick Wyatt
Senior Crafts Editor:
     Susan Ramey Cleveland
Senior Editor, Editorial Services:
     Olivia Kindig Wells
Art Director: James Boone

Christmas is Coming! Vol. 6

Editor: Catherine Corbett Fowler
Editorial Assistants: Catherine Barnhart Pewitt,
     Barzella Estle
Illustrator and Designer: Barbara Ball
Copy Editor: L. Amanda Owens
Senior Photographer: John O'Hagan
Photo Stylist: Connie Formby
Production and Distribution Director: Phillip Lee
Associate Production Manager: Theresa L. Beste
Production Assistant: Marianne Jordan Wilson
Publishing Systems Administrator: Rick Tucker

Contents

page 12

page 94

Children's Workshop: Happy Holiday Crafts

Parents' Workshop: Great Gifts for Children

page 118

A Note from the Editor

This year millions of people will be catching the spirit of the 1996 Olympic Games, which are being held right here in the USA. The excitement is spreading all over the world. Why, even the residents of the North Pole have decided to host their version of a grand sporting event. Right now the elves, the penguins, the snowmen, and Mr. and Mrs. Santa are preparing to watch their athletes—the reindeer—as they compete in the Reindeer Games! In the following pages, we invite you to be not only a spectator but also a participant in the festivities. Keep in mind that the athletes in these games are reindeer, who are part of *Santa's* team, so each event will have a definite Christmas feel to it.

Getting the most from this book:

Christmas is Coming is filled with crafting fun for the whole family. There are dozens of projects for you to make, and your parents will find lots of special things to make for you.

 In the first chapter, "Reindeer Games," you and your friends will discover projects relating to the biggest sporting event that takes place at the North Pole. There's even a special party section at the end of the chapter so you can host your own Reindeer Games.

 Our "Children's Workshop" chapter begins with "Trimmings to Fix." Here you'll find great projects to help you decorate your home or school for the holidays.

 Next in this chapter comes "Presents to Make," which is loaded with great gifts you can make for family and friends.

 Your mom will love the "Parents' Workshop" chapter, which begins with "Grin and Wear It." It contains a collection of fun clothes for kids.

 "Just for Fun," the last section in the third chapter, offers toys, totes, and more for grown-ups to make for you.

To make *Christmas is Coming* easier for you to use, we've divided the projects in "Reindeer Games" and "Children's Workshop" into three skill levels.

page 72

Level 1 projects are very basic. Even the youngest crafters should be able to make these with a little guidance.

Level 2 projects are slightly more involved and may require more time to make.

Level 3 projects are the most challenging. They may require a little assistance from a grown-up. They are good projects for older children.

page 48

Your safety is very important to us. When a project contains a step that should be done by or with the help of a grown-up, we make sure to tell you in bold print.

We hope you and your parents and teachers will enjoy making the projects in this book as much as we have enjoyed putting the book together for you. So gather your crafting supplies, because *Christmas is Coming!*

page 96

Your editor,

Catherine Corbett Fowler

Metric Conversion Chart

US Measurement	Metric Measurement
⅛"	3 mm
¼"	6 mm
⅜"	9 mm
½"	1.3 cm
⅝"	1.6 cm
¾"	1.9 cm
⅞"	2.2 cm
1"	2.5 cm
2"	5.1 cm
3"	7.6 cm
4"	10.2 cm
5"	12.7 cm
6"	15.2 cm
7"	17.8 cm
8"	20.3 cm
9"	22.9 cm
10"	25.4 cm
11"	27.9 cm
12"	30.5 cm
36"	91.5 cm
45"	114.3 cm
60"	152.4 cm
⅛ yard	0.11 m
¼ yard	0.23 m
⅓ yard	0.3 m
⅜ yard	0.34 m
½ yard	0.46 m
⅝ yard	0.57 m
⅔ yard	0.61 m
¾ yard	0.69 m
⅞ yard	0.8 m
1 yard	0.91 m

To Convert to Metric Measurements:

When you know:	Multiply by:	To find:
inches (")	25	millimeters (mm)
inches (")	2.5	centimeters (cm)
inches (")	0.025	meters (m)
feet (')	30	centimeters (cm)
feet (')	0.3	meters (m)
yards	90	centimeters (cm)
yards	0.9	meters (m)

Reindeer Games

Amid the clamor of Christmas carols, sleigh bells, and jolly bellows of "ho, ho, ho," a young reindeer holding a flashlight torch runs into the North Pole sporting arena to officially herald the start of the Reindeer Games!

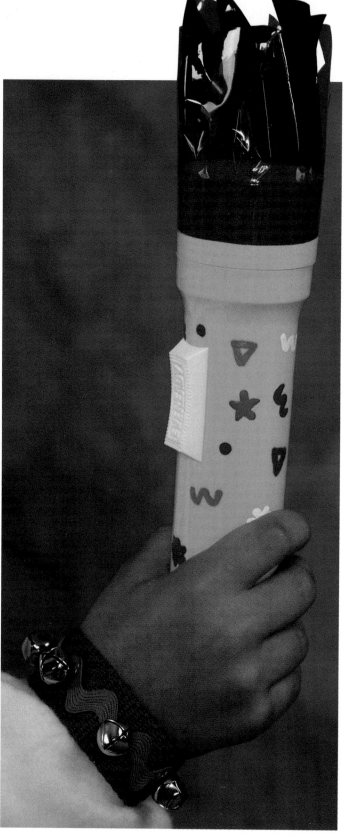

Flashlight Torch

Once the games are over, remove the cellophane flames and use the torch to light the way while Christmas caroling.

You will need:
A grown-up
Plastic disposable flashlight
Paint pens in variety of colors
Clear acrylic spray varnish
Tracing paper
Pencil
Scissors
Transparent tape
Cellophane: red, yellow

Note: We used red and yellow cellophane gift bags to make our flames.

1. Using the paint pens, randomly paint designs on the handle of the flashlight. Let the paint dry. **Ask the grown-up** to spray the handle with varnish. Let the varnish dry.

2. Using the pencil, trace the red and yellow flame patterns onto the tracing paper. Cut them out. Roll a piece of tape into a tube. Stick the tape circle on the back of the red flame pattern. Stick the pattern onto the red cellophane. Repeat to tape the yellow flame pattern onto the yellow cellophane. Cut out the red and yellow cellophane flames. Remove the paper patterns.

3. Tape the red flame to the light end of the flashlight. Tape the yellow flame on top of the red flame, positioning the points of the yellow flame between the points of the red flame.

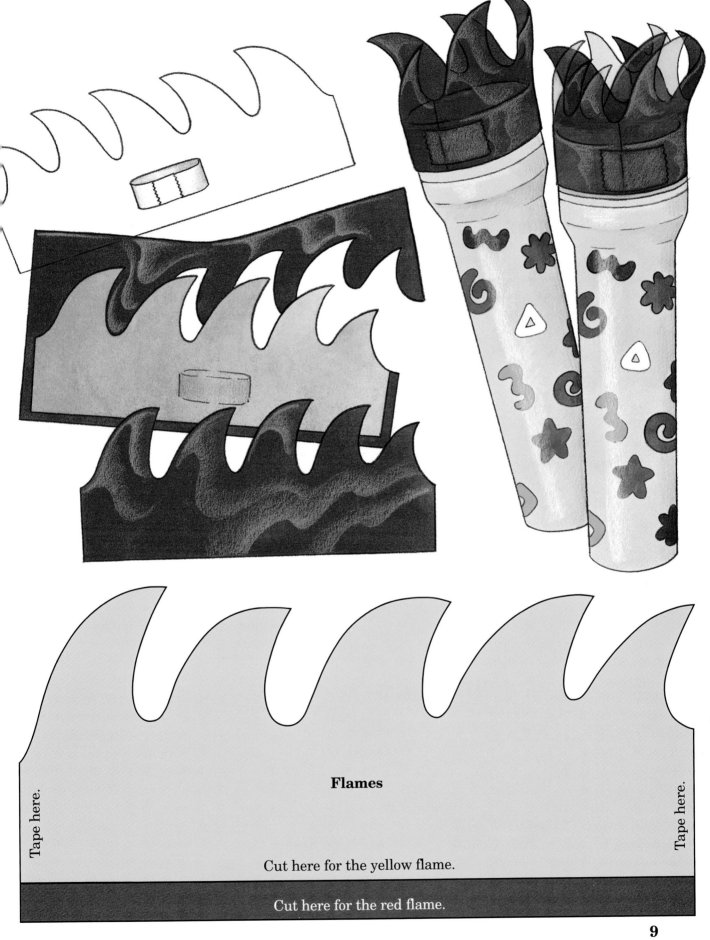

Flames

Tape here.

Tape here.

Cut here for the yellow flame.

Cut here for the red flame.

9

Five Golden Rings

Santa loves the shimmering symbol of the games, taken from a line in one of his favorite songs, "The Twelve Days of Christmas." An individual ring makes a bright holiday wreath.

You will need (for 1 wreath):
Ruler
Pencil
1 yard gold lamé
Scissors
40" length #6-gauge wire or wire clothes hanger
Pliers (for use with clothes hanger)
¾ yard 1"-wide ribbon
Craft glue

Note: You'll find a metric conversion chart on page 5.

1. Using the ruler and the pencil, measure and mark 1 (1" x 4") strip on the lamé. Cut out the strip. Using this strip as a pattern, cut the remainder of the lamé into strips.

2. If you are using a clothes hanger, untwist the hanger and straighten it with the pliers. Bend the clothes hanger or wire into a 10"-diameter circle, wrapping the ends of the wire around the circle to secure.

3. Positioning the ties very close together, tie each lamé strip into a knot around the wire. Be sure to pull the ends of each strip tightly.

4. Tie the ribbon into a bow. Glue the bow to the bottom of the wreath. Let the glue dry.

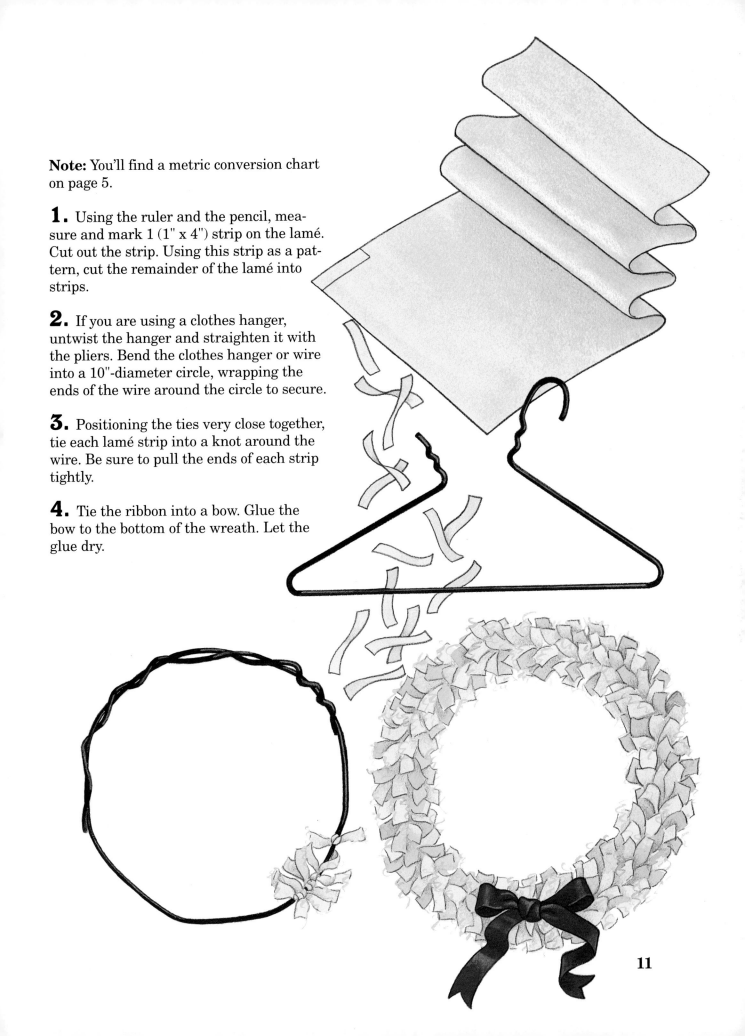

Reindeer Sweatshirts

The reindeer are divided into red, green, and blue teams. Each player wears a special sweatshirt that features his or her team color.

You will need (for 1 sweatshirt):
A grown-up
Peel-and-stick vinyl shelf covering
Ruler
Pencil
Scissors
Craft knife
Purchased white sweatshirt
Heavy cardboard (cut into the size of the
    sweatshirt front)
Thumbtacks
Spoon
Brush-on fabric paints: brown; red, green,
    or blue (depending on team color you
    choose); glitter gold
Pie tin
Stencil brush
Waxed paper
Small regular paintbrush
Iron and ironing board
Fabric paints in tube: white; red, green, or
    blue
3 gold star studs
Fabric glue
3 red, green, or blue 7-mm pom-poms

Note: Ask the grown-up to wash and dry
the sweatshirt before you begin. You'll find
a metric conversion chart on page 5.

1. Using the ruler and the pencil, measure
and cut 2 (6") squares and 1 (2½") square
from the vinyl shelf covering. Center and
transfer the reindeer pattern on page 15 onto
the **vinyl** side of 1 (6") square. Center and
transfer the reindeer pattern again to the
paper side of the remaining 6" square. Center and transfer the blanket pattern on page
15 onto the **vinyl** side of the 2½" square.

2. Ask the grown-up to use the craft
knife to cut out the reindeer head and body
on each 6" square and the blanket on the
2½" square.

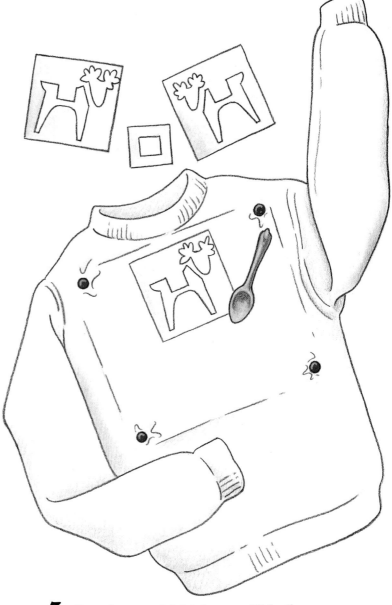

3. Lay the sweatshirt faceup. Slide the
cardboard inside the sweatshirt. Thumbtack the sweatshirt to the cardboard so
that the fabric is flat and secure. Select the
6" square with the reindeer facing to the
right when the paper side is down. Remove
the paper backing. Referring to the illustration, center the reindeer on the front of the
sweatshirt, 1¾" below the neckband. With
the sticky side down, press the square in
place. Use the back of the spoon to rub the
edges flat.

4. Squeeze a small amount of brown paint onto the pie tin. Dip only the bristles of the stencil brush into the paint. Dabbing from the edges of the reindeer stencil toward the middle, paint the reindeer. Carefully remove the stencil and place it on a sheet of waxed paper. Let the paint dry. Then stick the same stencil slightly below and to the **right** of the first reindeer. Paint this reindeer in the manner above. Carefully remove the stencil. Let the paint dry. For the final reindeer, use the remaining reindeer stencil. Remove the paper backing. Stick the stencil slightly below and to the **left** of the first reindeer (see the illustration). Paint the reindeer in the manner above. Carefully remove the stencil. Let the paint dry. Wash the stencil brush thoroughly.

5. Remove the paper backing from the 2½" square. Center the blanket stencil over the opening on 1 reindeer's back. Stick the stencil in place. Using the desired team color of brush-on paint, paint the blanket in the manner above. Carefully remove the stencil. Repeat to paint a blanket on each reindeer. Let the paint dry. Wash the stencil brush thoroughly.

6. Using the regular paintbrush and the glitter gold paint, paint the hoofs on each reindeer. Let the paint dry. Wash the brush thoroughly. **Ask the grown-up** to heat-set the paint on the sweatshirt, following the manufacturer's instructions.

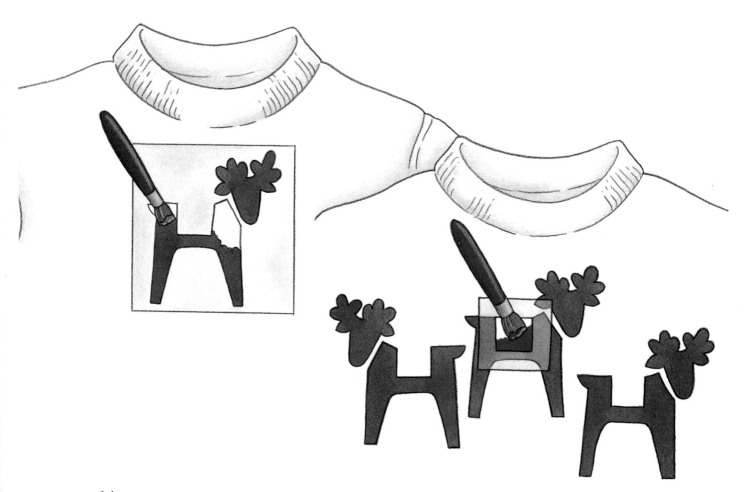

7. Using the white fabric paint, add 2 dots to the reindeer face for eyes. Alternating the white fabric paint and the desired team color of fabric paint, outline the sides and the bottom of the blanket with dots. Let the paint dry.

8. Ask the grown-up to center 1 star stud on each reindeer's blanket, pushing the tabs through to the wrong side of the sweatshirt. Using the tip of a pair of blunt scissors and working from the back, press the tabs toward the center of each stud.

9. Using the fabric glue, glue 1 pom-pom nose to each reindeer. Let the glue dry.

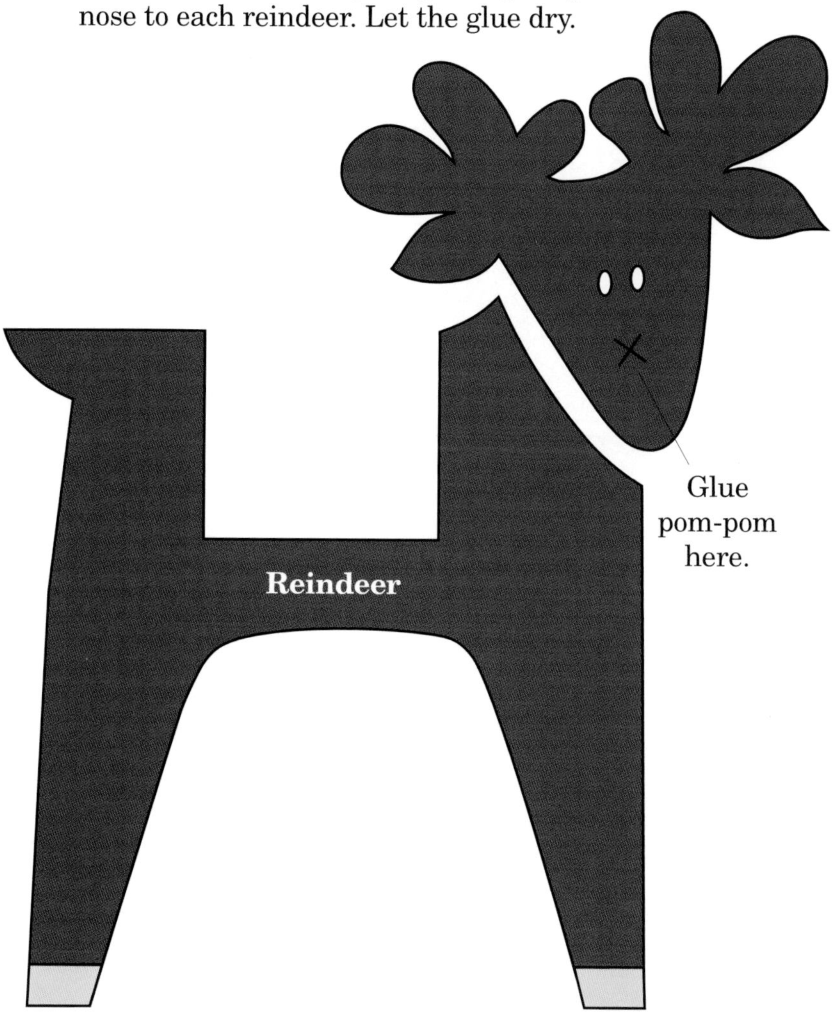

Glue
pom-pom
here.

Reindeer

Blanket

×
Attach star
stud here.

Jingle Bell Bracelets

As part of their team uniform, our reindeer athletes wear these jingle bell bracelets in place of sweatbands. After the games are over, they'll be great accessories for Christmas outfits.

You will need (for 1 bracelet):
9" length 1"-wide red or blue nylon belting
Thick craft glue
2 clothespins
9" length green rickrack
1" piece ½"-wide Velcro
5 (½"-diameter) jingle bells

Note: You'll find a metric conversion chart on page 5.

1. Turn each cut end of the belting under ½". Glue them in place. Clamp the glued ends with the clothespins until dry.

2. On the right side of the belting, glue the rickrack along the center, wrapping the cut ends of the rickrack to the wrong side. Let the glue dry.

3. Glue the hook half of the Velcro to the **right side** of the belting at 1 end. Glue the loop half of the Velcro to the **wrong side** of the belting at the opposite end. Let the glue dry.

4. Evenly space the jingle bells along the rickrick on the right side of the bracelet. Glue the jingle bells in place. Let the glue dry.

Holiday Hats

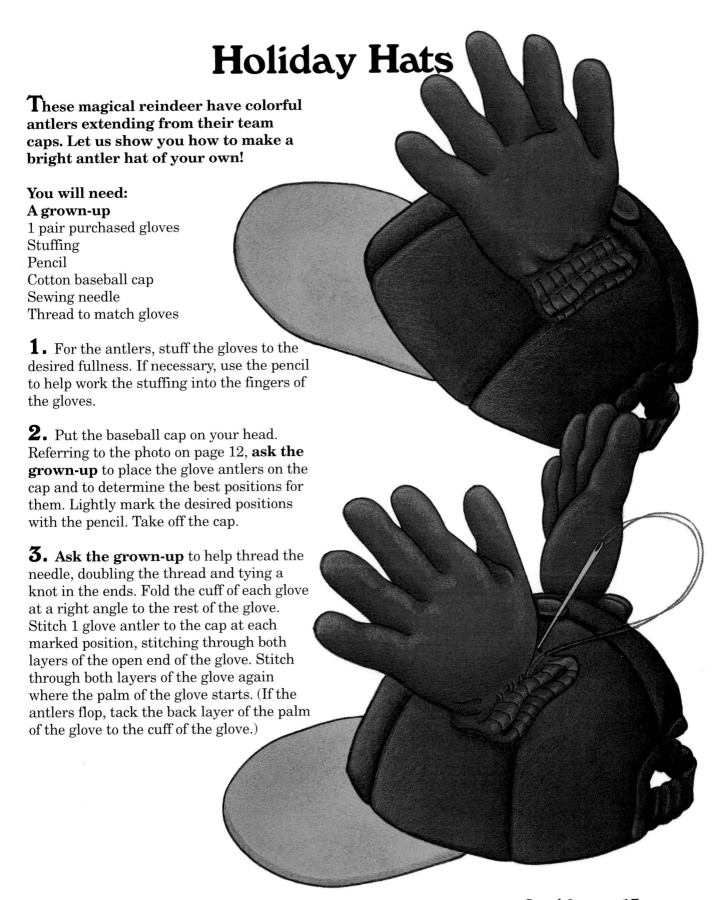

These magical reindeer have colorful antlers extending from their team caps. Let us show you how to make a bright antler hat of your own!

You will need:
A grown-up
1 pair purchased gloves
Stuffing
Pencil
Cotton baseball cap
Sewing needle
Thread to match gloves

1. For the antlers, stuff the gloves to the desired fullness. If necessary, use the pencil to help work the stuffing into the fingers of the gloves.

2. Put the baseball cap on your head. Referring to the photo on page 12, **ask the grown-up** to place the glove antlers on the cap and to determine the best positions for them. Lightly mark the desired positions with the pencil. Take off the cap.

3. **Ask the grown-up** to help thread the needle, doubling the thread and tying a knot in the ends. Fold the cuff of each glove at a right angle to the rest of the glove. Stitch 1 glove antler to the cap at each marked position, stitching through both layers of the open end of the glove. Stitch through both layers of the glove again where the palm of the glove starts. (If the antlers flop, tack the back layer of the palm of the glove to the cuff of the glove.)

Antlered Greetings

Dear
Santa,
Merry
Christmas
Joe

Christmas Card Designing is a very
important event at the Reindeer Games.
Imagine how proud our competitor is
to be able to say that he designed this
gold medal-winning card!

You will need (for 1 card):
Tracing paper
Pencil
Scissors
1 sheet brown construction paper
2" square red paper
Craft glue
5" square tan felt
Dimensional paints: black, white
Purchased envelope to fit card

Note: You'll find a metric conversion chart on page 5.

1. Using the pencil, trace the reindeer pattern on page 20 onto the tracing paper. Cut out the pattern. Transfer the reindeer pattern to the brown construction paper twice. Cut out each reindeer.

2. On 1 reindeer, cut out the nose area and the area inside the antlers, being careful **not** to cut into the areas from an outside edge.

3. Center and glue the red paper square to the wrong side of the nose opening. Let the glue dry.

4. Place 1 reindeer on the felt and trace around the antlers only. Cut out the felt antlers. Glue the felt antlers to the wrong side of the antler openings. Let the glue dry.

5. Refer to the photo to paint the following: Use the black paint to outline the antler and nose openings and to draw the reindeer head shape. Add 2 black blobs of paint above the nose to make the eyes. Let the paint dry. Add a dot of white paint to the center of each black eye. Add a circle of white paint around the outside of each black eye. Use the white paint to draw a wavy line down the center of each felt antler. Let the paint dry.

19

Inner Antlers
Cut out.

Reindeer

Nose
Cut out.

6. With the edges aligned, glue the remaining reindeer shape to the back of the decorated reindeer. Let the glue dry.

7. Write your message on the back of the reindeer card. Slip the greeting card into the envelope.

Critter Ornaments

The North Pole is home to some of the best Christmas tree decorators in the world, so you can imagine how very fierce the competition is in this tree-trimming event. This year the winning tree celebrated the animals of the North Pole competing in their favorite wintertime sporting events. See page 25 for instructions to make a matching tree skirt!

You will need (for each ornament):
Pencil
Tracing paper
Pinking shears
Scissors
Fabric glue
7" length small red rickrack
2 (7-mm) wiggle eyes
For the skiing bear: 5½" x 7½" scrap white, 4½" x 5" scrap gold, 2" x 4" scrap brown, 2" square green, and 3½" x 4" scrap red felt; 1 (½"-diameter) red and 1 (¼"-diameter) black pom-poms; 2" length black pearl cotton; 1¼" length small white rickrack
For the skating penguin: 5½" x 7½" scrap white, 4" x 4½" scrap black, 1" square yellow, and 1" x 3" scrap red felt; 2 (½"-diameter) red and 2 (¼"-diameter) green pom-poms; 3" length green and 6" length black small rickrack
For the snowshoeing bunny: 5½" x 7½" scrap green, 4" x 6½" scrap white, 3" x 3½" scrap gold, 2½" x 3" scrap red, and 2" square pink felt; 2" length black pearl cotton; 5" length small green rickrack
For the tobogganing reindeer: 6" x 8½" scrap white, 5" x 8" scrap brown, 3" x 4" scrap green, 3" x 5" scrap red, and 1" x 3" scrap black felt; 1 (¼"-diameter) black pom-pom; 2" length black pearl cotton; 1½" length small white rickrack

For the snowboarding seal: 5" x 7" scrap green, 4½" x 6" scrap gray, and 3½" x 4" scrap red felt; 1 (¼"-diameter) black and 1 (½"-diameter) green pom-poms; 2" length black pearl cotton; 2½" length white, 1½" length green, and 1" length yellow small rickrack

Note: You'll find a metric conversion chart on page 5.

Skiing Bear
1. Using the pencil, transfer the individual patterns on page 28 for the background, the bear body, the shoes, the skis, the ski poles, the scarf, the hat, and the ears to the tracing paper. Cut out the patterns. Transfer the patterns to the color felt indicated. Using the pinking shears, cut out the background. Using the regular scissors, cut out the other pieces. Cut along the ends of the red scarf piece to make the fringe.

2. Referring to the pattern for placement and leaving a border of the white background, glue the left ski in place. Glue the right ski in place, overlapping the left ski. Glue the bear body in place. Continue gluing in the following order: the shoes, the ski poles, the scarf, and the hat. Glue the ears on top of the hat. Let the glue dry.

3. Glue the red pom-pom on the hat between the ears. Glue the wiggle eyes just below the hat. Center and glue the black pom-pom nose below the eyes. Trim the pearl cotton and shape it into a mouth. Glue the mouth in place. Cut the white rickrack in half. Glue 1 piece across the tip of each ski as shown, trimming if necessary. To make the hanger loop, fold the red rickrack in half. Glue the cut ends to the back of the ornament at the top. Let the glue dry.

Skating Penguin

1. Using the pencil, transfer the individual patterns on page 29 for the background, the penguin body, the tummy, the beak, and the skates to the tracing paper. Cut out the patterns. Transfer the patterns to the color felt indicated. Using the pinking shears, cut out the background. Using the regular scissors, cut out the other pieces.

2. Referring to the pattern for placement and leaving a border of the white background, glue the penguin body in place on the background. Continue gluing in the following order: the tummy, the skates, and the beak. Let the glue dry.

3. Glue the eyes in place. To make the earmuffs, glue the green rickrack in an arch above the head; then glue the red pom-poms on each side of the head, covering the ends of the green rickrack. Glue 1 green pompom on top of each skate toe. Cut the black

rickrack in half. To make the ice skates blades, glue the black rickrack beneath each skate, trimming if necessary. To make the hanger loop, refer to Step 3 on page 22.

Snowshoeing Bunny

1. Using the pencil, transfer the individual patterns on page 28 for the background, the bunny body, the sweater, the heart, the nose, the inner ears, the snowshoe tops, and the snowshoe bottoms to the tracing paper. Cut out the patterns. Transfer the patterns to the color felt indicated. Using the pinking shears, cut out the background. Using the regular scissors, cut out the other pieces.

2. Referring to the pattern for placement and leaving a border of the green background, glue the snowshoe bottoms in place on the background. Glue the bunny body in place. Continue gluing in the following order: the snowshoe tops, the sweater, the heart, the nose, and the inner ears. Let the glue dry.

3. Glue the wiggle eyes on each side of the nose. Trim the pearl cotton and shape it into a mouth. Glue the mouth in place. Glue the green rickrack along the bottom, the neck, and the cuffs of the sweater, trimming to fit. To make the hanger loop, refer to Step 3 on page 22.

Tobogganing Reindeer
1. Using the pencil, transfer the individual patterns on page 29 for the background, the reindeer body, the 4 hooves, the scarf, and the toboggan to the tracing paper. Cut out the patterns. Transfer the patterns to the color felt indicated. Using the pinking shears, cut out the background. Using the regular scissors, cut out the other pieces. Cut along the ends of the green scarf piece to make the fringe.

2. Referring to the pattern for placement and leaving a border of the white background, glue the toboggan in place on the background. Glue the reindeer body in place; then glue the hooves and the scarf. Let the glue dry.

3. Glue the wiggle eyes and the black pom-pom nose in place. Trim the pearl cotton and shape it into a mouth. Glue the mouth in place. Glue the white rickrack along the left end of the toboggan, trimming if necessary. Roll the right end of the toboggan up and glue to hold. To make the hanger loop, refer to Step 3 on page 22.

Snowboarding Seal
1. Using the pencil, transfer the individual patterns on page 28 for the background, the seal body, the snowboard, and the hat to the tracing paper. Cut out the patterns. Transfer the patterns to the color felt indicated. Using the pinking shears, cut out the background. Using the regular scissors, cut out the other pieces.

2. Referring to the pattern for placement and leaving a border of the green background, glue the snowboard in place on the background. Glue the seal body in place; then glue the hat on top of the seal head. Let the glue dry.

3. Glue the green pom-pom at the tip of the hat. Glue the white rickrack along the front edge of the hat, trimming if necessary. Glue the wiggle eyes just below the hat. Center and glue the black pom-pom nose just below the eyes. Trim the pearl cotton and shape it into a mouth. Glue the mouth in place. Glue the yellow rickrack along the left end of the snowboard, trimming if necessary. Glue the green rickrack along the right end of the snowboard, trimming if necessary. To make the hanger loop, refer to Step 3 on page 22.

Critter Cloth

You will need (for 1 tree skirt):

A grown-up

Tracing paper

Pencil

Scissors

Felt: 1 (32"-diameter) circle and 5½" x 9"
  scrap white; 4 (8½" x 11") sheets red; 3" x
  10" scrap blue; 5 (8½" x 11") sheets green;
  7½" x 8½" scrap gold; 8½" x 11" sheet
  brown; 5" x 7½" scrap black; 2" square
  pink; 4½" x 6" scrap gray; 1" square yellow

Disappearing-ink fabric marker

Ruler

Fabric glue

Pom-poms: 2 (¼"-diameter) and 1 (½"-
  diameter) green; 3 (½"-diameter) red; 3
  (¼"-diameter) black

10 (7-mm) wiggle eyes

Black pearl cotton

Small rickrack: 6" length white, 1" length
  yellow, 6" length black, 1¼ yard green

Sewing machine (optional)

Red thread (optional)

Straight pins

Note: You'll find a metric conversion chart on page 5.

1. Using the ruler and the fabric marker, measure and mark a 7"-diameter circle in the center of the 32"-diameter felt circle. Cutting from the outside edge, cut into the center of the white felt circle and cut out the 7"-diameter circle.

2. Refer to the instructions for the ornaments to make individual patterns for each of the animal pieces, omitting the background piece for all except the bunny. Trace the patterns for the tree and the pennant (page 29) onto the tracing paper. Cut them out. Transfer the tree pattern to the green felt 5 times. Transfer the pennant pattern to the green, red, and blue felt 5 times each. Cut out the trees and the pennants. Transfer the animal patterns to the color felt indicated. Cut out the pieces, stacking the pieces for each animal seperately.

3. Positioning the penguin's right wing 3¼" from the left cut edge of the white felt circle and the bottom of the penguin body 3" from the bottom edge, glue the penguin body to the white circle. Referring to steps 2 and 3 on page 23, assemble the penguin. Glue 1 tree to the white felt circle 1½" from the penguin's left wing and 1¾" from the bottom edge of the circle. Referring to the illustration for placement and the ornament instructions on pages 22—24 for assembly, continue gluing animals and trees to the white felt circle, spacing them evenly. Let the glue dry.

4. Cut 2"-wide strips from the remaining red felt. **Ask the grown-up** to stitch the strips together, using a ¼" seam allowance, to make 1 (2" x 144") strip. Or if you prefer to do this step yourself, overlap the ends of the strips ¼" and glue them together to make 1 (2" x 144") strip. Let the glue dry.

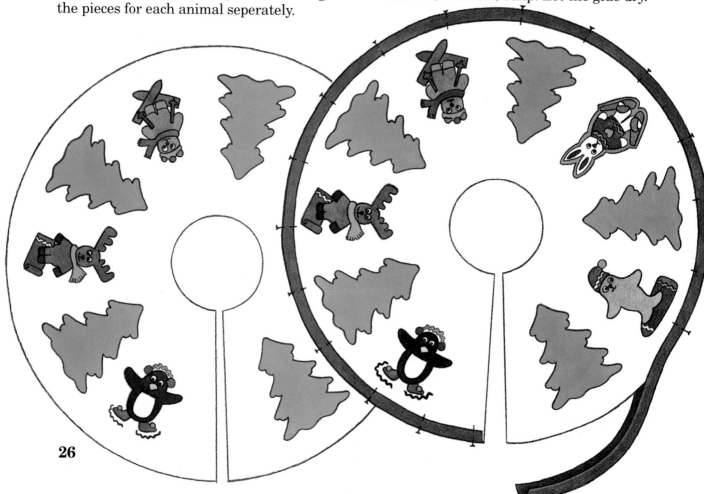

5. **Ask the grown-up** to fold the strip in half and encase the outside edge of the circle, holding the strip in place with pins. Trim to fit. Using the red thread and setting the sewing machine for a zigzag stitch, stitch along the cut edges of the red felt strip to bind the outside edge of the circle. Make sure to catch both the top and bottom layers of the red felt strip. Or if you prefer, glue the red felt strip to the outside edge of the circle, trimming to fit. Be sure to glue both the top and bottom layers of the strip. Let the glue dry. Repeat this step to bind the edge of the center circle; then bind the straight edges of the tree skirt opening.

6. Referring to the photo, make the line of pennants around the center of the tree skirt, gluing green rickrack 1½" from the center opening and trimming to fit. Beginning 1" from the left cut edge of the opening, glue 1 green pennant in place with the top straight edge touching the bottom edge of the rickrack circle. Glue 1 blue pennant ½" to the left of the green pennant; then glue 1 red pennant ½" to the left of the blue pennant. Continue gluing pennants around the rickrack circle, alternating green, blue, and red. Let the glue dry.

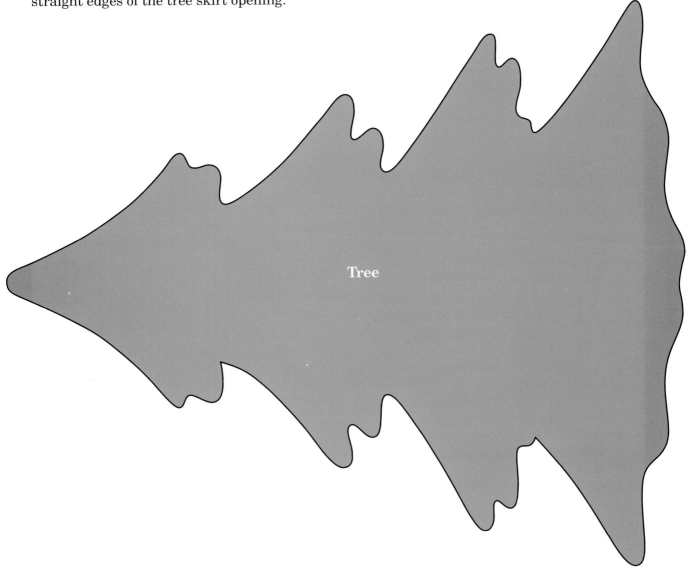

Tree

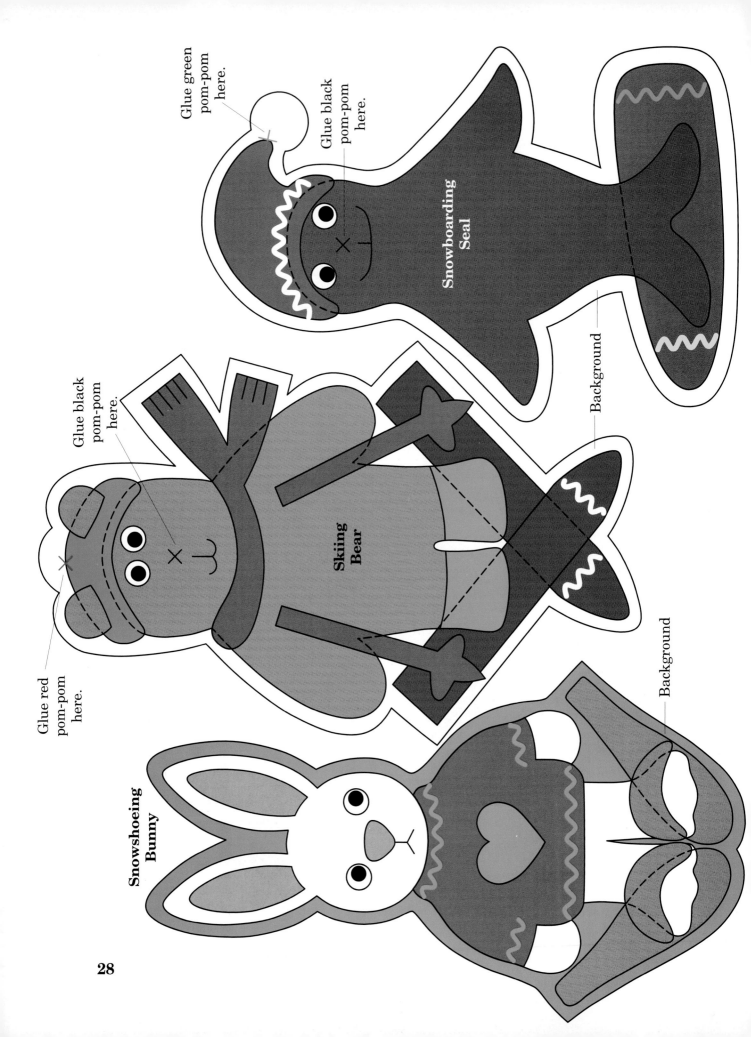

Glue green pom-pom here.

Glue black pom-pom here.

Snowboarding Seal

Background

Glue black pom-pom here.

Glue red pom-pom here.

Skiing Bear

Background

Snowshoeing Bunny

28

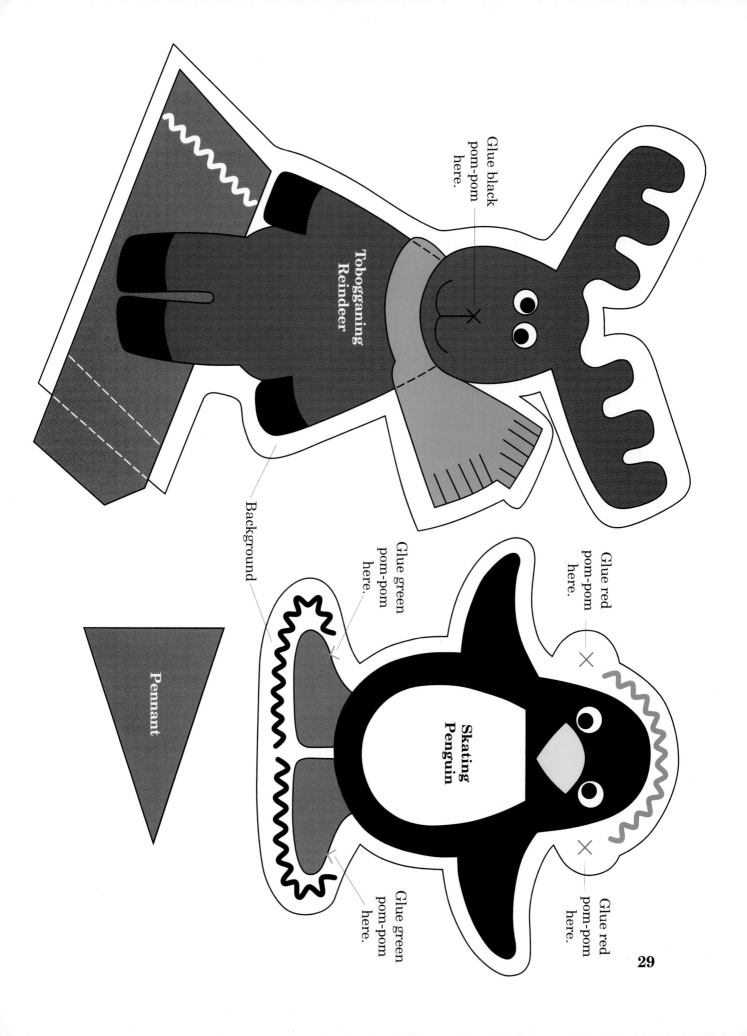

Glue black
pom-pom
here.

Tobogganing
Reindeer

Background

Glue green
pom-pom
here.

Glue red
pom-pom
here.

Glue red
pom-pom
here.

Pennant

Skating
Penguin

Glue green
pom-pom
here.

29

Layered Felt Stocking

Requiring very strong organizational skills, the Stocking Stuffing Competition challenges the athletes to stuff the most goodies inside in the shortest amount of time. Here we present the official stocking for this year's competition.

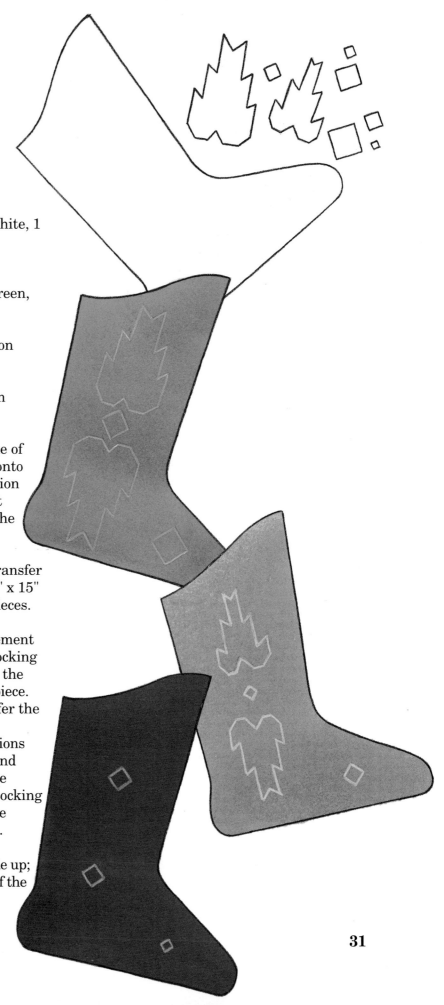

You will need (for 1 stocking):
Tracing paper
Pencil
Scissors
White fabric marker
12" x 15" felt rectangles: 2 green, 2 white, 1
   gold, 1 red
Straight pins
Embroidery needle
#8 pearl cotton embroidery thread: green,
   gold, red
Embroidery scissors
6" length ½"-wide red grosgrain ribbon
1 red star button

Note: You'll find a metric conversion
chart on page 5.

1. Using the pencil, trace the outline of
the stocking pattern on pages 34-35 onto
the tracing paper and trace each section
of the stocking design separately. Cut
out the stocking and each section of the
design.

2. Using the white fabric marker, transfer
the outline of the stocking to each 12" x 15"
felt rectangle. Cut out the stocking pieces.

3. Referring to the pattern for placement
of the design and positioning each stocking
piece with the toe to the right; center the
largest sections on 1 green stocking piece.
Using the white fabric marker, transfer the
outline of the sections. Remove these
pieces. Center the medium-sized sections
on the gold stocking piece. Transfer and
then remove these pieces. Position the
smallest design sections on the red stocking
piece. Transfer and then remove these
pieces. These lines are stitching lines.

4. With the outlined sections right side up;
pin the marked green stocking on top of the

31

gold stocking, aligning the edges. Thread the embroidery needle with 1 strand of the green pearl cotton and tie a knot in the end. Starting from underneath, push the needle through both layers of the pinned stockings, positioning the needle so that it pierces the outer line of 1 section on the green stocking piece. Pushing the needle up and down through the felt, stitch along this line. When you return to the beginning, tie off the pearl cotton and trim the end. Repeat for each remaining section on the green stocking piece.

5. Pull the green felt away from the gold felt in the center of each design. Using the embroidery scissors, cut through the green felt **only.** Trim the green felt close to the inside of the stitching line to reveal the gold felt.

6. With the outlined section right side up, pin the red felt stocking piece underneath the gold stocking piece, aligning the edges. Thread the embroidery needle with 1 strand of the gold pearl cotton and tie a knot in the end. Stitching in the previous manner, stitch along the outlined sections, tying off and trimming the pearl cotton when you reach the end of each. Trim the gold felt from the inside of each design in the previous manner to reveal the red felt.

7. Pin 1 white felt stocking piece underneath the red stocking piece, aligning the edges. Thread the embroidery needle with the red pearl cotton and tie a knot in the end. Stitching in the previous manner, stitch along the outlined sections, tying off and trimming the pearl cotton when you reach the end of each. **(Note:** The diamond in the center of the stocking does not have a stitching line. Therefore the felt should not be trimmed.) Trim the red felt from the inside of each design in the previous manner to reveal the white felt.

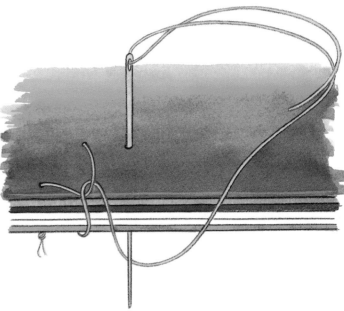

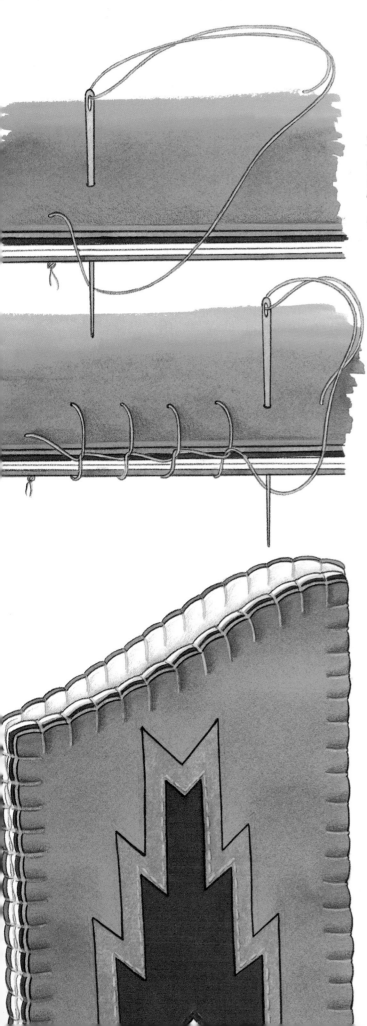

8. Stack the remaining white stocking piece on top of the remaining green stocking piece, aligning the edges. Pin the stitched stocking pieces faceup on top of the white/green stocking pieces. (A green stocking piece should be on the top and the bottom.) Thread the embroidery needle with 1 strand of the gold pearl cotton and tie a knot in the end. Beginning at 1 top side edge, blanket-stitch along the sides and the bottom of the stocking, stitching through all the layers. Do **not** stitch the top edge yet.

Referring to the drawings, to make a blanket stitch, bring the needle up at Point 1 (the cut edge of the stocking). Insert the needle at Point 2 (on top of the stocking), which is slightly above and to the right of Point 1. Push the needle through to Point 3, which is directly below Point 2 and to the right of Point 1. The pearl cotton should be under the needle. Push the needle all the way through. Point 3 is now Point 1 for the next stitch. Work the next stitch in the same manner. Continue to the opposite top edge. Tie off the pearl cotton and trim the end.

9. At the top open edge of the stocking, separate the top 4 layers from the bottom 2. Blanket-stitch the top 4 layers together in the previous manner; then blanket-stitch the bottom 2 layers together.

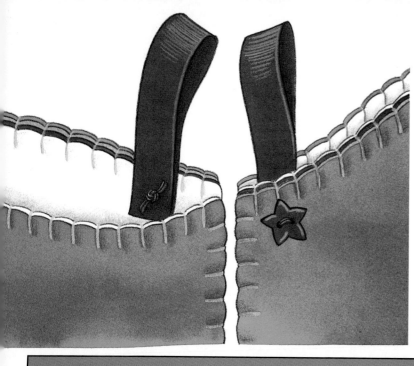

10. To make the hanging loop, fold the ribbon in half, aligning the cut edges. Place 1" of the cut ends inside the stocking at the left top edge. Using 1 strand of the red pearl cotton and knotting the end, stitch the ribbon to the front layers of the stocking. Tie off the end of the pearl cotton and trim. Referring to the illustration, stitch the button to the front of the stocking, just below the hanging loop.

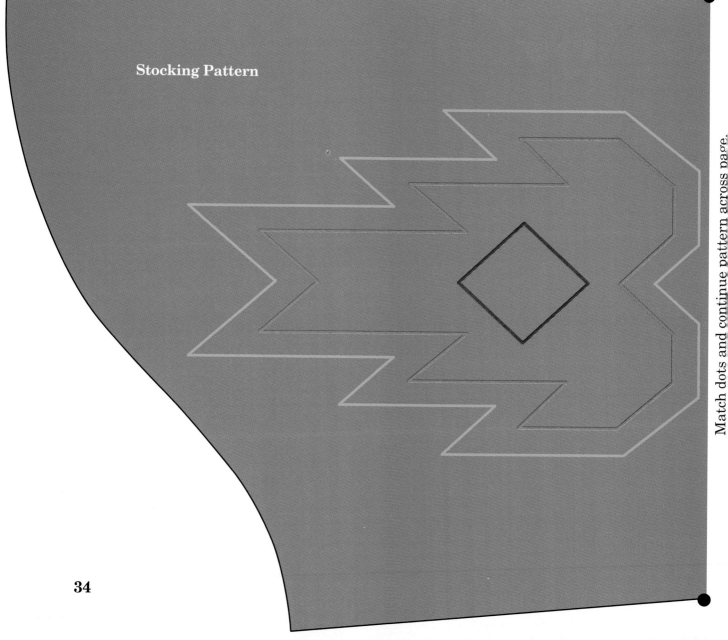

Stocking Pattern

Match dots and continue pattern across page.

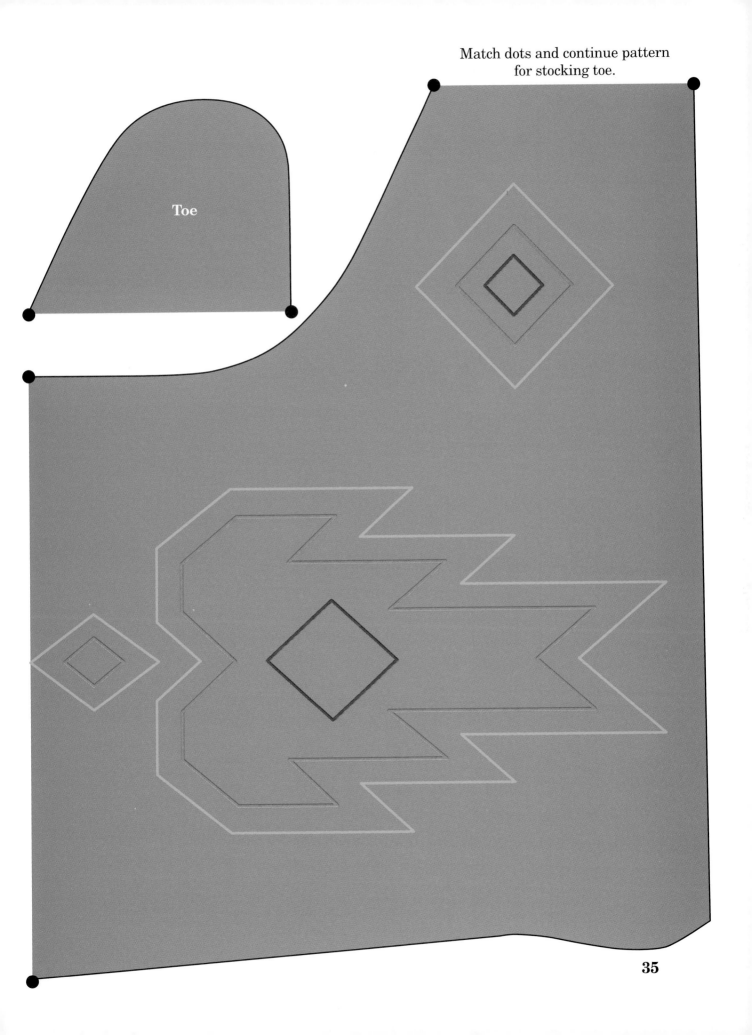

Match dots and continue pattern
for stocking toe.

Toe

Ribbon Wand

The elves are very interested in the winning design for the Toy Designing Competition. They know that they will be making hundreds of this gold medal-winning toy.

You will need:
A grown-up
8 (1-yard) lengths 1"-wide satin ribbon
8 (⅝"-diameter) white plastic rings
Thick craft glue
8 clothespins
36" length ⅝"-diameter wooden dowel
Red enamel spray paint
1 (⅝"-diameter) white rubber furniture
　leg tip
1 eye screw
1 key ring

Note: You'll find a metric conversion chart on page 5.

1. For each ribbon, thread 1" of 1 cut end through 1 plastic ring. Spread the glue on the back of the 1" section and press to the back of the ribbon. Hold it in place with a clothespin until the glue is dry.

2. Ask the grown-up to help you spray-paint the dowel red. Let the paint dry. Slip the rubber tip onto 1 end of the dowel. Screw the eye screw into the top center of the opposite end.

3. Slide the ribbon-threaded plastic rings onto the key ring. Then attach the key ring to the eye screw.

4. This toy is intended for outside use. Hold the dowel and run, letting the ribbons stream through the air behind you. Or stand still and, holding the dowel, wave the ribbons through the air and watch the swirling shapes they create.

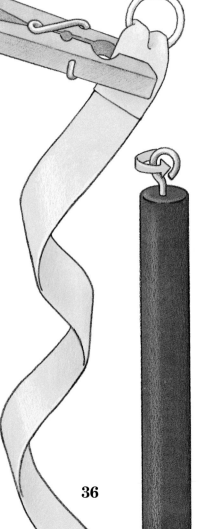
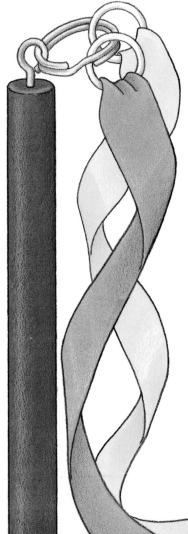

36

Level 2

Gold Medal Door Decoration

Each athlete who wins an event has his or her bedroom door draped with a giant gold medal. (The award plate can proclaim any job well done — from Best Room Cleaner to Good Grades Champ!)

You will need:
A grown-up
1 (10½"-diameter) heavy-duty paper plate
Red permanent marker
Gold glitter glue
3 yards 2"-wide gold metallic streamer
Stapler and staples
Thick craft glue
Scissors
1¼ yards 45"-wide blue fabric
Liquid ravel preventer
6 thumbtacks
1 rubber band
1 straight pin

Note: You'll find a metric conversion chart on page 5.

1. Using the marker, write the award message on the back of the plate. Decorate the back with glitter glue. Let the glue dry.

2. **Ask the grown-up** to help you fold and staple the metallic streamer into 1" pleats.

3. Glue the pleated streamer to the back of the decorated plate around the outer edge. Let the glue dry. Set the plate aside.

4. Cut the fabric in half. Apply the liquid ravel preventer to the cut edges. **Ask the grown-up** to center 1 short end of 1 fabric rectangle on 1 top corner of the door. Thumbtack it in place. Thumbtack each of the top corners of the rectangle to the edges of the door. Repeat with the remaining rectangle, securing it to the opposite top corner.

5. Gather the 2 rectangles of fabric together at the center of the door. Hold the rectangles together with the rubber band.

6. **Ask the grown-up** to center the decorated plate over the rubber band and, using the straight pin, carefully pin the top of the pleated ribbon to the fabric.

Olympic-Sized Party

The Christmas season is a great time to host your own Reindeer Games. Call all your friends, tell them to don their favorite holiday sports-wear, then gather for a fun-filled afternoon of friendly competition and tasty treats.

SILLY SPORTS

Weather permitting, play these games outdoors. If you must stay indoors, be sure to move furniture and breakable items out of the way.

5 GOLDEN RINGS

Five golden rings are the official symbol of the Reindeer Games (see the project on page 10). This game puts a twist on that symbol. Before the party, have **a grown-up** spray-paint 5 Hula-Hoops® gold. Let the paint dry thoroughly.

To play the game, select 5 participants. Have each of them place a Hula-Hoop around his or her waist. When **the grown-up referee** gives the signal, all players begin to hula-hoop. If someone drops the ring, that player is out. Continue until only 1 person remains in the game. If there are only 5 partygoers, this person is the winner. If there are more than 5 people attending the party, have this first group sit down and let the next group begin to hula-hoop. The winner of this group must compete with the winner of the first group to determine the overall winner.

Present the winner with a special gold Christmas ornament. Give the second-place winner a special silver Christmas ornament.

GARLAND RELAY

Place 2 small tables at the end of a room. Put a pile of 6"-long brightly colored tinsel pipe cleaners. Divide the participants into 2 teams.

To play the game, have all the players stand behind a masking tape line placed at a designated distance from the tables. When **the grown-up referee** gives the signal, 1 person from each team runs to the table and shapes 1 pipe cleaner into a circle, twisting the ends together to secure. He or she leaves the pipe cleaner circle on the table as soon as he or she is finished and runs back across the line. The next person from that team then runs to the table, picks up another pipe cleaner, inserts the second pipe cleaner into the first, and twists it into a circle to begin to form a garland. The game continues in this manner until a predetermined amount of time has passed. When the time is up, the team that has made the longest garland wins.

For their golden first-place award, give each member of the winning team a gold foil-wrapped chocolate drop. Give each member of the second-place team a silver foil-wrapped chocolate drop.

REINDEER RINGTOSS

This event requires a little preparty preparation. You will need to have **a grown-up** help you. Gather a medium-sized cardboard box, black and red permanent markers, 2 sticks with several branches extending from them, scissors, masking tape, and 3 plastic lids, such as those found on tubs of margarine.

On 1 end of the box, draw the basic shape of a reindeer head, using the black marker. Add eyes and a mouth. Using the red marker, draw a round nose.

Ask **the grown-up** to poke a hole in each top corner of the decorated end of the box. Insert the end of 1 stick through each hole so that the branches look like antlers. Keep the sticks in place by taping the ends to the inside of the box.

To make the rings to toss, ask **the grown-up** to cut out the center of each plastic lid, making sure they do **not** cut into the center from an outside edge.

Place the box on a table so that the end with the antlers extends off the edge of the table. Place several books inside the box to hold it in place. Place a masking tape line on the floor at a designated distance from the reindeer box.

To play the game, have the first participant stand behind the masking tape line. Give this person the 3 plastic rings. Have the player toss the rings and see how many he can hang on the antlers. The game continues until each participant has had a turn. If several players tie, let them have a "toss-off" until there is 1 only champion.

Award the first-place winner a goldfish in a small bowl and include a container of fish food. Present the second-place winner with a shiny silver dollar.

CONCESSION STAND

Before the games begin, between events, or after the closing ceremonies, be sure to head to the concession stand to indulge in these treats.

If you wish, you can post a list of snack selections. Simply make a menu board by writing with markers on posterboard.

THE TORCH

An ice-cream cone with a cotton candy flame

You will need (for 6 ice-cream cones):
6 (1-cup) scoops ice cream
Ice cream scoop
6 waffle ice-cream cones
Cotton candy: red, yellow

1. Place 1 scoop of ice cream in each waffle cone. Freeze the filled cones for 1 hour.

2. Just before serving, top each cone with shreds of red and yellow cotton candy to resemble a flame. Serve immediately.

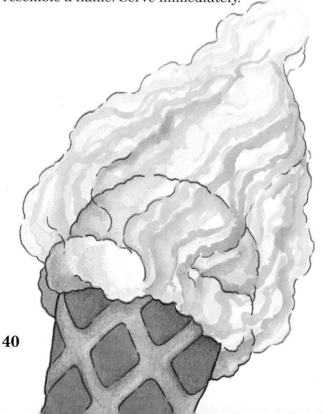

THE DISCUS

A thin tortilla sandwich with cheese and pepperoni

You will need (for 6 sandwiches):
A grown-up
⅓ cup mayonnaise
¼ cup grated Parmesan cheese
Dash of garlic salt
Small bowl
Spoon
12 (6") flour tortillas
1 cup shredded Cheddar cheese
30 slices pepperoni
Large nonstick skillet
Vegetable cooking spray

1. Combine the mayonnaise, the Parmesan cheese, and the garlic salt in the small bowl. Stir with the spoon until the mixture is blended.

2. Evenly divide the mayonnaise mixture on 6 tortillas. Use the back of the spoon to spread the mixture into a thin layer on each.

3. Evenly sprinkle the Cheddar cheese over the mayonnaise mixture. Arrange the pepperoni slices on top. Then cover with the remaining 6 tortillas, pressing gently.

4. Ask the grown-up to coat the skillet with the cooking spray. Place the skillet over medium-high heat until hot. Cook the tortilla sandwiches, 1 at a time, 1 to 2 minutes on each side until they are browned and the cheese is melted. Serve hot.

RINK-SIDE FREEZE
A fruited frozen treat on a stick

You will need (for 24 freezes):
24 (3-ounce) paper drinking cups
13" x 9" x 2" baking pan
2 (6-ounce) cans frozen pineapple juice
    concentrate, thawed
1 (16-ounce) carton low-fat vanilla yogurt
Medium-sized bowl
Spoon
6 cups of seedless red or green grapes
24 wooden craft sticks
Heavy-duty plastic wrap (optional)
Curly ribbon (optional)

1. Place the drinking cups in the pan.

2. Combine the pineapple juice concentrate and the yogurt in the bowl. Stir until blended. Pour the mixture into the drinking cups, filling each two-thirds full. Place the pan in the freezer for 30 minutes.

3. Remove the pan from the freezer. Place 4 to 6 grapes in each cup, pressing them

gently into the yogurt mixture. Freeze for an additional 30 minutes.

4. Insert 1 stick into the center of each cup until it almost reaches the bottom. Freeze for 4 hours.

5. If desired, wrap each Rink-Side Freeze in heavy-duty plastic wrap and tie it with curly ribbon. The freezes can be made in advance and frozen for up to 2 weeks.

THE SQUEEZE PLAY
*A creamy filling squeezed between 2 layers
of a brownie*

You will need (for 12 brownie treats):
A grown-up
1 (21.5-ounce) box brownie mix
Wire rack
Plastic wrap
Knife
1 (12-ounce) container frozen whipped
    topping, thawed
Tablespoon
Heavy-duty plastic wrap

1. Ask the grown-up to prepare the brownie mix according to the directions on the box for cakelike brownies. Cool the brownies completely on the wire rack. Cover the brownies with plastic wrap and chill them in the refrigerator for 1 hour. **Ask the grown-up** to cut the brownies into 12 squares; then slice each brownie in half sideways.

2. Place a heaping tablespoon of the whipped topping on the bottom half of 1 split brownie. Cover it with the top half of the split brownie. Wrap the filled brownie in heavy-duty plastic wrap and freeze. Brownies can be made in advance; once wrapped they can be stored for up to 2 weeks.

Childrens' Workshop

Happy
Holiday
Crafts

Glowing Globes

Jazz up glass hurricane globes with dimensional paint. When a globe is placed over a lit candle, the painted designs cast cool patterned shadows on the table.

You will need (for each globe):
1 purchased glass hurricane lamp globe
1 votive candle
For the polka dot globe: silver glitter and blue dimensional paints
For the zigzag globe: red and green dimensional paints

Note: Be sure to use silver glitter *paint*. There is also a silver glitter *glue* available that looks like the paint, but the glue will melt and run when the globe is placed over a lit candle. You'll find a metric conversion chart on page 5.

1. **For the polka dot globe,** with the globe upright, paint dots randomly over the entire surface, using the silver and blue paints (see the photo). Let the paint dry approximately 12 hours. Place the globe over the lit votive candle.

2. **For the zigzag globe,** with the globe upright, use the red paint to paint a zigzag around the top of the globe. Referring to the photo and alternating the red and green paints, paint a ring of dots beneath the red zigzag. Paint a green zigzag beneath the dots. Leave approximately 2" beneath the green zigzag and paint a red zigzag and a green zigzag. Leave a space of approximately 1" and then repeat as above, ending with a red zigzag, a ring of red and green alternating dots, and a green zigzag. Let the paint dry approximately 12 hours. Place the globe over the lit votive candle.

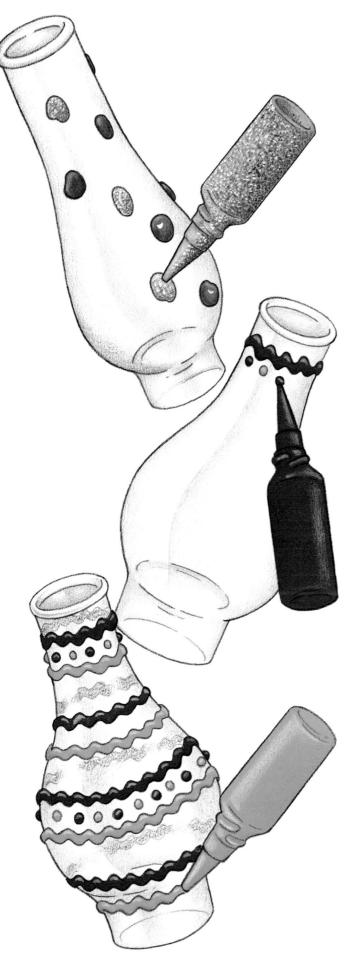

Glittery Snowflakes

Note: You'll find a metric conversion chart on page 5.

1. Cut the bottom out of the plastic berry basket. Trim this bottom piece to the desired snowflake shape.

2. Place the plastic snowflake on a sheet of waxed paper. Coat 1 side with the glue. Sprinkle glitter on top of the glue. Place the snowflake on the bottom half of the open egg carton. Let the glue dry. Repeat to apply glitter to the other side of the snowflake.

3. For the hanger, tie the gold string or cord around 1 prong of the snowflake. Tie the ends of the string together in a knot.

These sparkly ornaments are a quick-and-easy recycling project. The snowflake base is made from the bottom of a plastic berry basket.

You will need (for 1 snowflake ornament):
Plastic berry basket
Scissors
Waxed paper
Craft glue
Glitter in desired color
Foam egg carton
6" gold thread or gold cord for hanger

Hard Candy Christmas

Bright candies are not just for eating—they're also good for decorating. By gluing them to a coffee can, you can create a colorful vase.

You will need:
2 rubber bands
5"-diameter coffee can
Thick craft glue
Approximately 36 candy sticks
1 yard 1"-wide green polka-dot grosgrain ribbon
Flowers or small potted Christmas tree

Note: You'll find a metric conversion chart on page 5.

1. Place the rubber bands around the coffee can, positioning 1 near the top and 1 near the bottom. Apply glue to 1 side of 1 candy stick. Slip the candy stick under the rubber bands, with the glue side toward the can. Continue in this manner until the can is covered. Let the glue dry.

2. Remove the rubber bands. Tie the ribbon in a knot around the center of the candy-covered can. Fill the vase with water and flowers or a small Christmas tree.

Wintertime Waders

Sloshing through wintery slush is fun when your boots are decorated for the season. And because these boots are stenciled, you don't have to be an expert to paint them.

You will need (for each pair):
A grown-up
Peel-and-stick vinyl shelf covering
Scissors
Pencil
Craft knife
Paintbrush
Paper plate
Clear acrylic spray varnish
White brush-on acrylic paint
For the candy cane boots: purchased
    pair of red rubber boots
For the snowman boots: purchased pair
    of rubber boots in desired color, black
    and yellow paint pens

Note: You'll find a metric conversion
chart on page 5.

1. Cut out a 2" x 3" piece from the vinyl
covering. Use the pencil to trace the
desired stencil on page 50 onto the paper
side of this piece. **Ask the grown-up** to
cut out the outlined areas of the stencil,
using the craft knife.

2. For the candy cane boots, peel the
paper backing off the candy cane stencil.
Stick the stencil along the top edge of 1
boot. Rub to make sure that all the edges
adhere to the boot.

3. Squirt a blob of white paint onto the
paper plate. Dip the paintbrush into the
paint. Paint over the stencil, making sure
that the paint does not extend beyond the
edges of the stencil. Carefully peel off the
stencil. Continue placing and painting in
this manner to stencil candy canes around
the top edge of both boots, making sure
that the edges of the stencil do not touch
any painted candy canes. Let the paint dry.
Wash the paintbrush.

4. **Ask the grown-up** to spray a light coat of varnish over the stenciled candy canes to help keep the paint from flaking off. Let the varnish dry.

5. **For the snowman boots,** peel the paper backing off the snowman stencil. Center and stick the stencil on the outer side of 1 boot (see the photo). Rub to make sure that all the edges adhere to the boot.

6. Squirt a blob of white paint onto the paper plate. Dip the paintbrush into the paint. Paint over the stencil, making sure that the paint does not extend beyond the edges of the stencil. Carefully peel off the stencil. Let the paint dry. Using the black paint pen and referring to the photo, paint eyes, a nose, and a mouth on the head of the snowman; then paint 4 round buttons down the center of the body and a top hat on the head. Using the yellow paint pen, paint the scarf around the neck. Let the paint dry. Repeat to paint a snowman on the outer side of the remaining boot.

7. **Ask the grown-up** to spray a light coat of varnish over the stenciled snowmen to help keep the paint from flaking off. Let the varnish dry.

Candy Cane

Snowman

50

Wire Stars

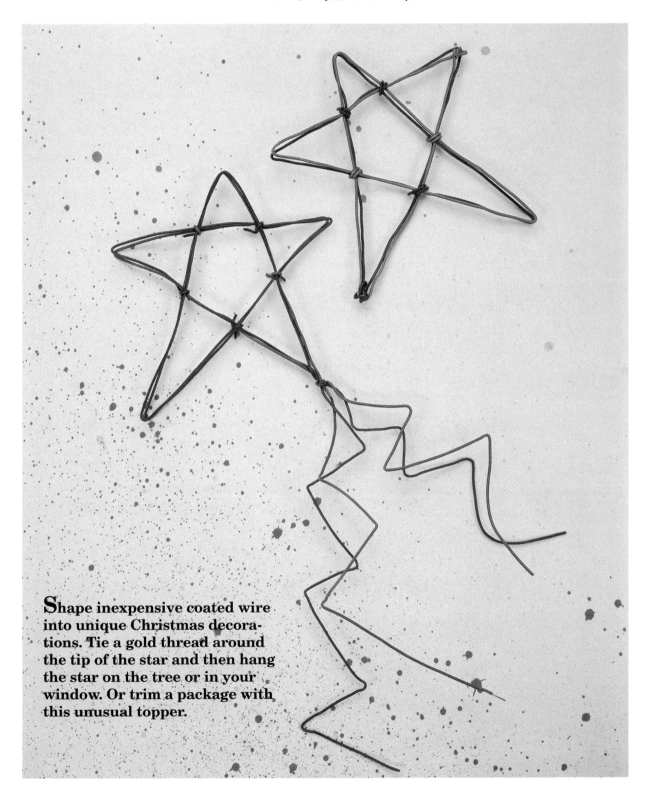

Shape inexpensive coated wire into unique Christmas decorations. Tie a gold thread around the tip of the star and then hang the star on the tree or in your window. Or trim a package with this unusual topper.

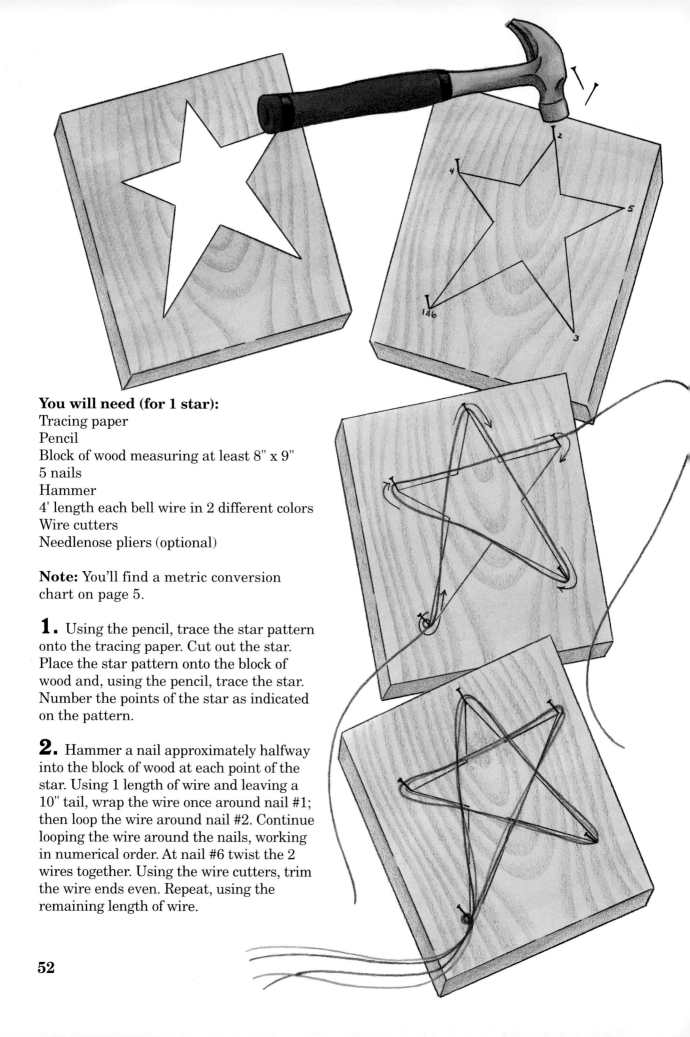

You will need (for 1 star):

Tracing paper
Pencil
Block of wood measuring at least 8" x 9"
5 nails
Hammer
4' length each bell wire in 2 different colors
Wire cutters
Needlenose pliers (optional)

Note: You'll find a metric conversion chart on page 5.

1. Using the pencil, trace the star pattern onto the tracing paper. Cut out the star. Place the star pattern onto the block of wood and, using the pencil, trace the star. Number the points of the star as indicated on the pattern.

2. Hammer a nail approximately halfway into the block of wood at each point of the star. Using 1 length of wire and leaving a 10" tail, wrap the wire once around nail #1; then loop the wire around nail #2. Continue looping the wire around the nails, working in numerical order. At nail #6 twist the 2 wires together. Using the wire cutters, trim the wire ends even. Repeat, using the remaining length of wire.

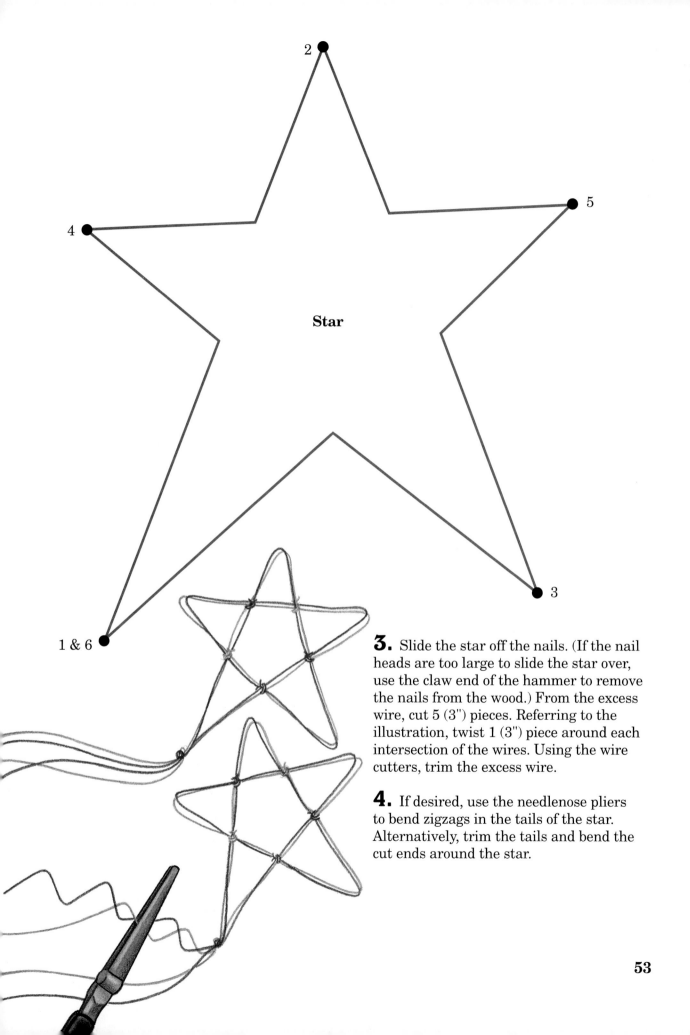

2

5

4

Star

3

1 & 6

3. Slide the star off the nails. (If the nail heads are too large to slide the star over, use the claw end of the hammer to remove the nails from the wood.) From the excess wire, cut 5 (3") pieces. Referring to the illustration, twist 1 (3") piece around each intersection of the wires. Using the wire cutters, trim the excess wire.

4. If desired, use the needlenose pliers to bend zigzags in the tails of the star. Alternatively, trim the tails and bend the cut ends around the star.

Golden Leaf Table Runner

Decorate your family's table with an elegant paper table runner—no sewing required!

You will need:
Ruler
Pen
36"-wide green craft paper
Transparent tape
Gold metallic water-based paint
Aluminum pie pan
Stiff paintbrush
Several sizes and varieties of leaves
Paper napkins
Hole punch
Raffia

Note: See Step 1 to determine amount of paper required. You'll find a metric conversion chart on page 5.

1. Measure the length of the table. Add 26" to this measurement. Cut a strip of craft paper equal to this measurement by 18" wide.

2. Fold each long edge of the craft paper strip under ½". Run the side of the pen along each fold to press the crease. Fold each short end under 1". On the back of the craft paper strip, mark the center of each short end. Measure and mark each long edge 8½" from each short end. Fold the corners at these marks to make a point at each end. Tape the corners to the back.

3. Squeeze gold paint into the pie pan. Using the paintbrush, apply a thin coat of paint on the underside of 1 leaf. (You may need to thin the paint *slightly* with water so that it will spread easily.) Place the leaf paint side down on the front of the runner. Cover the leaf with a napkin and press, being careful not to shift the leaf. Remove the napkin and gently lift off the leaf. (Each leaf may be reused many times.) Continue printing leaves on the table runner as desired.

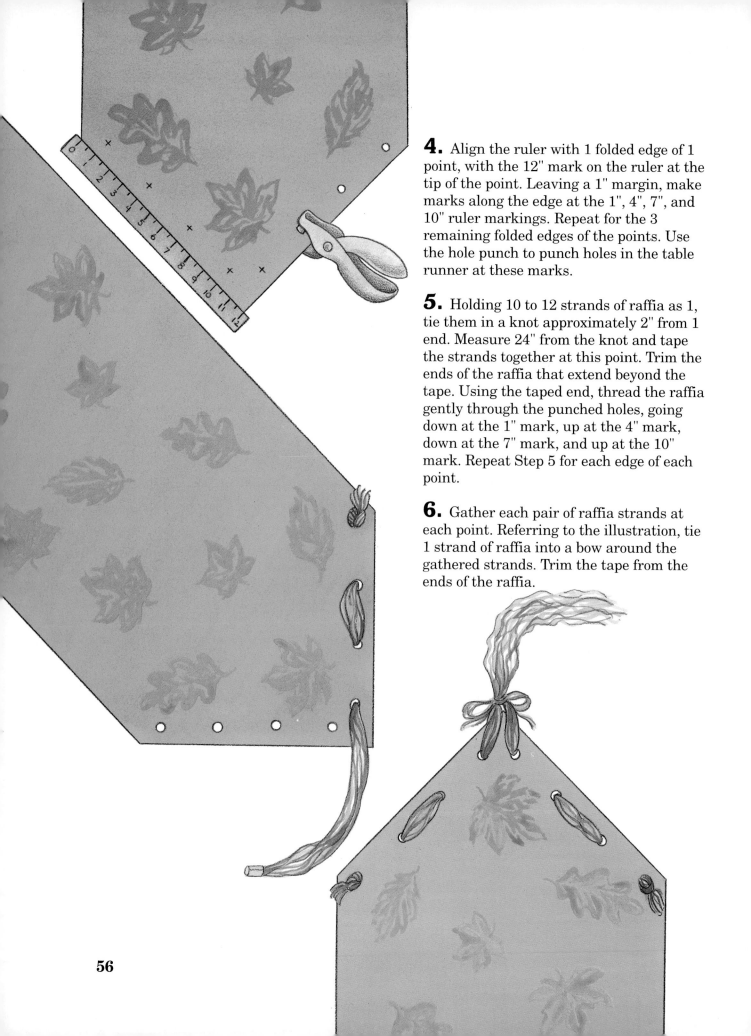

4. Align the ruler with 1 folded edge of 1 point, with the 12" mark on the ruler at the tip of the point. Leaving a 1" margin, make marks along the edge at the 1", 4", 7", and 10" ruler markings. Repeat for the 3 remaining folded edges of the points. Use the hole punch to punch holes in the table runner at these marks.

5. Holding 10 to 12 strands of raffia as 1, tie them in a knot approximately 2" from 1 end. Measure 24" from the knot and tape the strands together at this point. Trim the ends of the raffia that extend beyond the tape. Using the taped end, thread the raffia gently through the punched holes, going down at the 1" mark, up at the 4" mark, down at the 7" mark, and up at the 10" mark. Repeat Step 5 for each edge of each point.

6. Gather each pair of raffia strands at each point. Referring to the illustration, tie 1 strand of raffia into a bow around the gathered strands. Trim the tape from the ends of the raffia.

Holly Jolly Gift Wrap

Create unique crinkled wrapping by untwisting purchased twisted paper. Add a few big jingle bells to complete your "berry" special packaging.

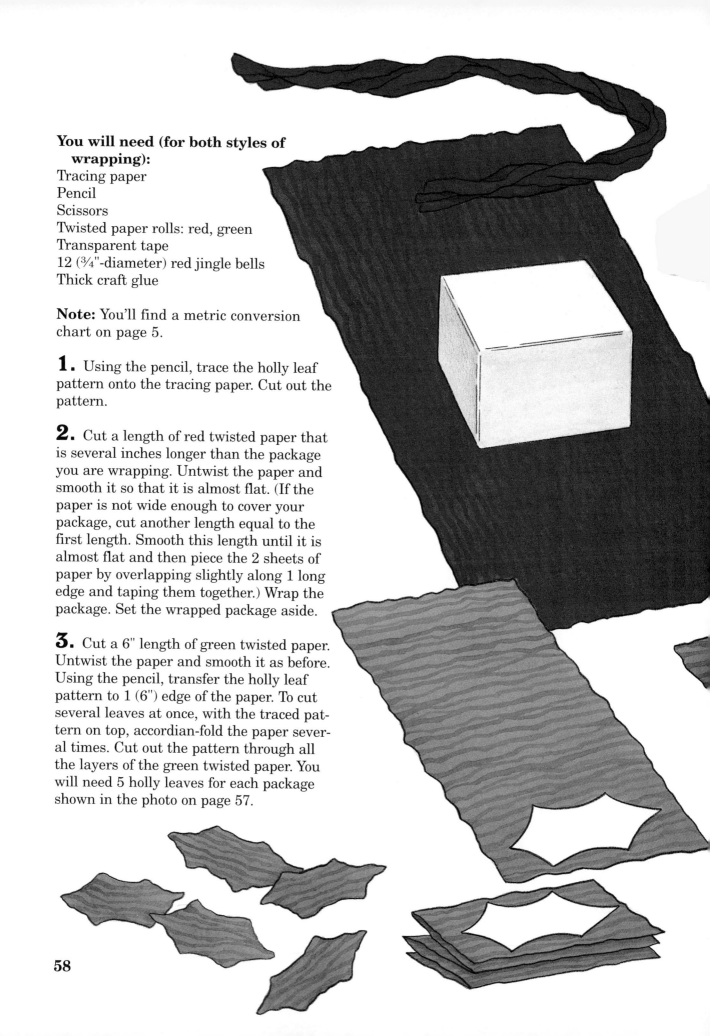

You will need (for both styles of wrapping):
Tracing paper
Pencil
Scissors
Twisted paper rolls: red, green
Transparent tape
12 (¾"-diameter) red jingle bells
Thick craft glue

Note: You'll find a metric conversion chart on page 5.

1. Using the pencil, trace the holly leaf pattern onto the tracing paper. Cut out the pattern.

2. Cut a length of red twisted paper that is several inches longer than the package you are wrapping. Untwist the paper and smooth it so that it is almost flat. (If the paper is not wide enough to cover your package, cut another length equal to the first length. Smooth this length until it is almost flat and then piece the 2 sheets of paper by overlapping slightly along 1 long edge and taping them together.) Wrap the package. Set the wrapped package aside.

3. Cut a 6" length of green twisted paper. Untwist the paper and smooth it as before. Using the pencil, transfer the holly leaf pattern to 1 (6") edge of the paper. To cut several leaves at once, with the traced pattern on top, accordian-fold the paper several times. Cut out the pattern through all the layers of the green twisted paper. You will need 5 holly leaves for each package shown in the photo on page 57.

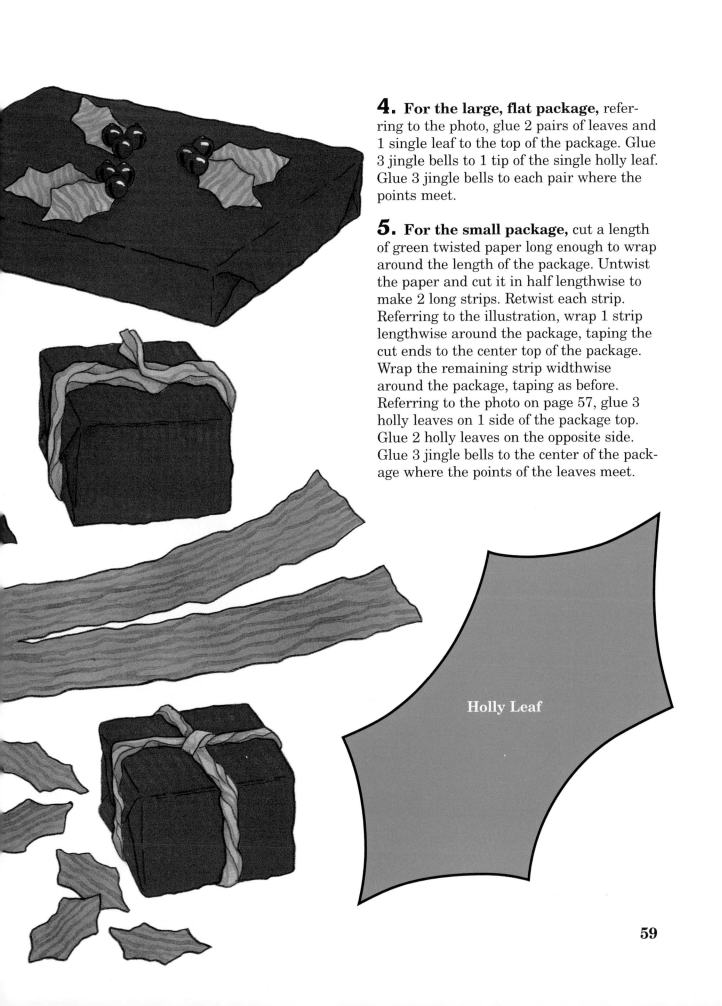

4. **For the large, flat package,** referring to the photo, glue 2 pairs of leaves and
1 single leaf to the top of the package. Glue
3 jingle bells to 1 tip of the single holly leaf.
Glue 3 jingle bells to each pair where the
points meet.

5. **For the small package,** cut a length
of green twisted paper long enough to wrap
around the length of the package. Untwist
the paper and cut it in half lengthwise to
make 2 long strips. Retwist each strip.
Referring to the illustration, wrap 1 strip
lengthwise around the package, taping the
cut ends to the center top of the package.
Wrap the remaining strip widthwise
around the package, taping as before.
Referring to the photo on page 57, glue 3
holly leaves on 1 side of the package top.
Glue 2 holly leaves on the opposite side.
Glue 3 jingle bells to the center of the package where the points of the leaves meet.

Holly Leaf

Seeing Stars

Follow our simple recipe for making spice dough stars and then decorate a pot, a package, or a tree with them.

You will need (for the basic Spice Dough Stars):
A grown-up
Large bowl
3 cups all-purpose flour
⅔ cup salt
1⅓ cups water
¼ cup cinnamon
3 tablespoons nutmeg
3 tablespoons ginger
3 tablespoons ground cloves
Dish towel
Baking sheet
Aluminum foil
Waxed paper
Rolling pin
2" metal star cookie cutter
Oven
Gold spray paint
Small paintbrush
Metallic acrylic paint in variety of colors
For the package toppers and the garland: coffee stirrer or small straw, twine, scissors
For the pot: clay flower pot in desired size, thick craft glue, hard candies or potted plant (optional)

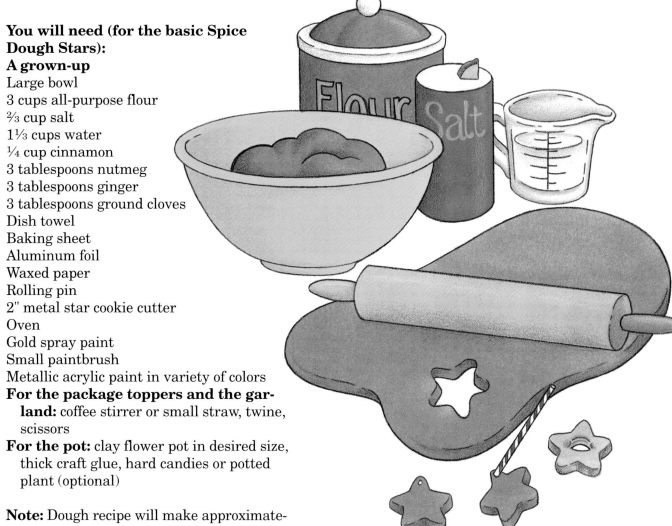

Note: Dough recipe will make approximately 48 (2") stars. The dough will smell good once it is mixed, but it should not be eaten. *Never* eat the painted stars. You'll find a metric conversion chart on page 5.

1. In the large bowl, mix the flour, the salt, and the water until a stiff dough forms. (You may need to use your hands.) Add the cinnamon, the nutmeg, the ginger, and the ground cloves to the dough and work them in. Roll the dough into a ball. Put the ball into the bowl. Cover the bowl loosely with the towel. Refrigerate the covered bowl for 1 hour. (Cold dough is easier to roll and to cut.)

2. Cover the baking sheet with aluminum foil. Place a small ball of the dough on a sheet of waxed paper. Roll the dough out to ½" thickness. Use the cookie cutter to cut out the star shapes. Place the cutout star shapes onto the baking sheet. Continue balling up and rolling out the dough until there is no more dough. (The more you handle the dough the harder it is to work with.)

3. For the package toppers and the garland, use the coffee stirrer or the straw to punch a hole in 1 point of each star.

4. Refrigerate all of the stars overnight. The next day, remove the stars from the refrigerator and let them sit and warm to room temperature. **Ask the grown-up** to preheat the oven to 250°. Bake the stars for 1 hour or until they look puffy. Let the stars cool completely.

5. Leave the stars on the aluminum foil and take them outside to spray-paint. **Ask the grown-up** to help you spray-paint 1 side of each star with the gold paint. Let the paint dry. Turn each star over and paint the other side. Let the paint dry.

6. Using the paintbrush and the metallic acrylic paints, paint a colored star on the top of each dough star (see the illustration). Let the paint dry.

7. For the package toppers, cut a length of twine and tie it around your package. Cut another length of twine and thread several stars onto the twine, tying a knot after each star. Tie this twine around the length already on the package.

8. For the garland, cut a length of twine slightly longer than you want the finished garland to be. Thread 1 star onto the twine and slide it to the opposite end. Tie a knot in the twine at the top of the star. Repeat with another star approximately 6" from the first star. Continue in this manner along the entire length of the twine.

9. For the pot, ask the grown-up to help you spray-paint the clay pot with the gold paint. Let the paint dry. Coat the center back of 1 star with thick craft glue. Stick the star onto the outside of the pot. Continue gluing stars to the pot as desired. Let the glue dry. If desired, fill several small pots with individually wrapped hard candies or fill a large pot with a potted plant.

Measuring Tree

Record how much you have grown between one Christmas and the next by painting your name and height along with the year on a felt ornament. Then hang the ornament at the appropriate measurement—bet you'll be surprised at how quickly you reach the top boughs of the tree!

You will need:
Tracing paper
Pencil
Scissors
Felt: ½ yard each 45"-wide green and red; 12" square blue; 3½" x 10½" piece yellow; 5" x 10½" piece black
Pinking shears
Measuring tape
Plaid™ Tacky Glue
1½ yards yellow jumbo rickrack
17" length ¼"-diameter wooden dowel
28" length white yarn
Plaid™ White Fashion Fabric Paint

Note: We recommend the glue and the paint listed above because the paint bottle has a fine tip that makes writing easier, and the glue will not seep through the felt and show on the right side. You'll find a metric conversion chart on page 5.

Level 2

1. Fold a sheet of tracing paper in half. With the long straight edge of the pattern on the fold, using the pencil, trace the triangle tree pattern on page 66 onto the tracing paper. Cut out the triangle. Trace the star pattern onto a single layer of the remaining tracing paper. Cut out the star. Unfold the tracing paper triangle and transfer it to the green felt 5 times. Transfer the star to the blue felt 1 time.

2. Using the pinking shears, cut a 13½" x 45" piece from the red felt. Using the regular scissors, cut out the felt triangles and the star. Cut 3 (3"-diameter) circles each from the red, blue, and yellow felt. Cut 9 (1" x 1¾") rectangles and 1 (5" x 6") rectangle from the black felt.

3. Apply a line of glue along 1 short end of the 13½" x 45" red felt piece. Fold the glued end over 3" and hold in place until the glue sticks. This is the top of the growth chart. Turn the growth chart over.

4. Refer to the illustration to glue the following: Center and glue the 5" x 6" black felt rectangle to the front of the growth chart, with 1 (6") edge 1½" from the bottom edge of the chart. Center and glue 1 green triangle on top of the black rectangle, overlapping the top of the rectangle by 1½". Center and glue another triangle on top of the first triangle, overlapping the tip of the first triangle by 2". In the same manner, continue centering and gluing the remaining triangles. Center and glue the star on top of the tree. Let the glue dry.

5. Referring to the illustration for placement, cut lengths of yellow rickrack and glue 1 to each triangle. Let the glue dry.

6. To make the ornaments, glue 1 (1" x 1¾") black rectangle to each circle, with the long edges horizontal and half of the rectangle extending off the edge.

7. Measure 6" from the bottom edge of the chart. Using the fabric paint, paint a dot ¾" from the right edge of the chart at this point. Measure 6" from this point and mark with a dot. Paint "3" next to this dot. Continue in this manner, measuring and marking at 6" intervals, to designate the 4' and 5' levels (see illustration). Let the paint dry.

8. Run the dowel through the casing. Center the growth chart on the dowel. Tie 1 end of the yarn to the dowel next to 1 edge of the growth chart. Tie the remaining end of the yarn to the dowel next to the opposite edge of the growth chart.

9. Ask the grown-up to hang the growth chart on a wall 2' above the floor; then ask him or her to measure you. Using the fabric paint, paint your name, your height, and the year on 1 ornament. Let the paint dry. Glue the ornament to the tree at the appropriate measurement.

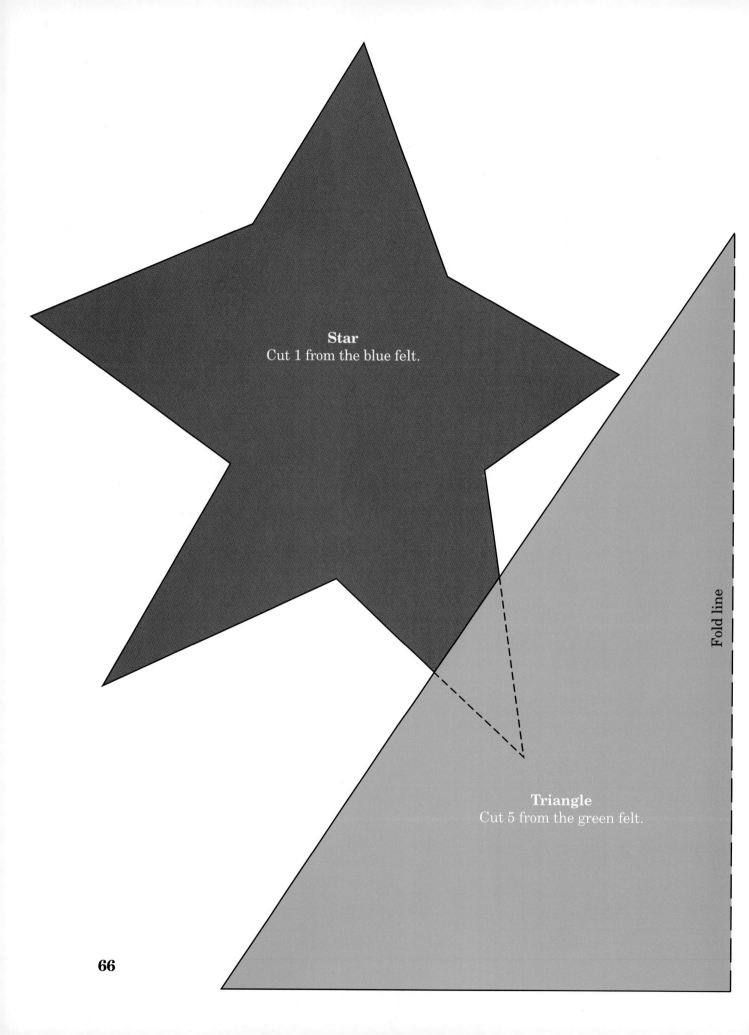

Star
Cut 1 from the blue felt.

Triangle
Cut 5 from the green felt.

Fold line

North Pole Finger Puppets

Act out the story of Rudolph or Frosty or create your own Christmas tale with these cheery mini puppets made from plush felt.

You will need (for each puppet):
Tracing paper
Pencil
Scissors
Thick craft glue
Ruler
2 (7-mm) wiggle eyes
For Santa: 4" x 6" scrap red plush felt; 3" x 3½" scrap white, 1½" x 3" scrap red, and 1½" x 2" scrap flesh-colored regular felt; 1 (7-mm) white and 2 (5-mm) black pom-poms; fine-tip permanent black marker
For Mrs. Santa: 4" x 6" scrap red plush felt, 2½" square white and 2" square flesh-colored regular felt, 5 (5-mm) white pom-poms, fine-tip permanent black marker, pink cosmetic blush, cotton swab
For the reindeer: 4" x 6" scrap tan plush felt, 2½" x 3½" scrap tan regular felt, 1 (7-mm) red pom-pom, 1 green pipe cleaner
For the snowman: 4" x 6" scrap white plush felt; 1¾"-diameter circle white, 2" x 2½" scrap green, and 1½" square orange regular felt; 3 (5-mm) black pom-poms; fine-tip permanent black marker

Note: You'll find a metric conversion chart on page 5.

Basics For All Puppets:
Using the pencil, trace the desired patterns on page 70 onto the tracing paper. Cut them out. Transfer the patterns to the colors of felt indicated. Cut out the puppet pieces.

Apply a thin line of glue along the sides and the top of 1 body piece. With the edges aligned, glue the 2 body pieces together, leaving the straight bottom edge unglued. Let the glue dry.

Santa
1. Refer to Basics to glue the body pieces together. Then glue the head/beard piece onto the body, with the bottom of the piece 1¼" above the bottom edge of the body. Glue Santa's hat in place. Center and glue Santa's face below the hat. Let the glue dry.

2. Referring to the illustration, glue the white pom-pom to the tip of the hat. Center and glue the black pom-poms on Santa's body. Glue the wiggle eyes in place, leaving ¼" between the eyes. Using the black marker, draw a smile below the face piece. Let the glue dry before using the puppet.

Mrs. Santa

1. Refer to Basics to glue the body pieces together. Glue Mrs. Santa's head/hair piece onto the body, with the bottom of the head 2" above the bottom edge of the body. Glue the face along the bottom of the head. Let the glue dry.

2. Referring to the illustration, glue the wiggle eyes ⅜" from the top of the face, leaving ¼" between the eyes. Using the black marker, draw a smile. Glue the white pom-poms in a curve below the face, spacing them evenly. Let the glue dry.

3. To make Mrs. Santa's cheeks, using the cotton swab, apply the blush to the face on each side of the mouth.

Reindeer

1. Cut the pipe cleaner into 2 (3") pieces. Fold each piece in half. Glue the bent pipe cleaners to the center top of 1 body piece, with the bent ends extending ½" beyond the edge of the felt. Let the glue dry.

2. Refer to Basics to glue the body pieces together, making sure that the pipe cleaners are sandwiched between the body pieces. Glue the head in place, with the bottom of the head 1¾" above the bottom edge of the body. Let the glue dry.

3. Referring to the illustration, glue the wiggle eyes ¾" above the bottom of the face, leaving ½" between the eyes. Glue the red pom-pom at the bottom center of the face. Let the glue dry before using the puppet.

Snowman

1. Refer to Basics to glue the body pieces together. Glue the 1¾"-diameter circle to the top of the body, with the bottom of the circle 2¼" above the bottom edge of the body.

2. Referring to the illustration, glue the hat on the top of the head, angling it slightly. Center and glue the wiggle eyes below the hat, leaving ⅜" between the eyes. Glue the nose below the eyes, with the straight end centered between the eyes. Using the black marker, draw a smile below and to the right of the nose. Center and glue the black pom-poms in a row on the body. Let the glue dry before using the puppet.

Santa Head/Beard
Cut 1 from white regular felt.

Santa Hat
Cut 1 from red regular felt.

Santa Face
Cut 1 from flesh-colored regular felt.

Puppet Body
Cut 2 for each puppet.
Snowman – white plush felt
Reindeer – tan plush felt
Santa and Mrs. Santa – red plush felt

Mrs. Santa Head/Hair
Cut 1 from white regular felt.

Reindeer Head
Cut 1 from tan regular felt.

Mrs. Santa Face
Cut 1 from flesh-colored regular felt.

Snowman Hat
Cut 1 from green regular felt.

Snowman Nose
Cut 1 from orange regular felt.

Pom-pom Gift Tags

Puffy pom-poms say it all! These gift tags are perfect for personalizing any package.

You will need (for each gift tag):
Pencil
1 sheet Fun Foam in desired color
Craft glue
13-mm pom-poms in desired colors
Scissors
Hole punch
24" length jumbo rickrack or ½"-wide grosgrain ribbon in desired color

Note: You'll find a metric conversion chart on page 5.

1. Using the pencil, print the desired name on the Fun Foam, making sure to leave ample space between each letter.

2. Outline the first letter with glue. Position pom-poms in the glue to form the shape of the letter. Continue in this manner with the remaining letters. Let the glue dry.

3. Very lightly draw a rectangle on the Fun Foam around the pom-pom name, making sure that each edge of the rectangle is at least 1" from the pom-pom name. Referring to the photo, make 1 short end of the rectangle come to a point. Cut out the gift tag.

4. Punch a hole in 1 short end of the gift tag. Thread the rickrack or the ribbon through the hole. Tie the gift tag to a package.

Ring in the Holidays

These colorful napkin rings make it easy to add Christmas cheer to your table. Whip up a set in no time.

You will need (for 2 tree and 2 star napkin rings):

Tracing paper

Pencil

Scissors

Fun Foam: 2½" x 7¼" scrap red, 7" x 7¼" scrap blue, 5" square green, 4½" square yellow

Stapler and staples

Rhinestones: 1 each gold and purple stars; 2 each small red, green, gold, blue, and purple circles; 1 each red and blue diamonds

Craft glue

1. Using the pencil, trace the tree and star patterns onto the tracing paper. Cut out the patterns. Cut 2 (1¼" x 7¼") strips each from the red and blue foam. Transfer the tree pattern to the green foam 2 times. Transfer the star pattern to the blue and yellow foam 1 time each. Cut out the trees and the stars.

2. Fold each 1¼" x 7¼" strip into a circle, overlapping the ends slightly. Staple the ends together. Set the circles aside.

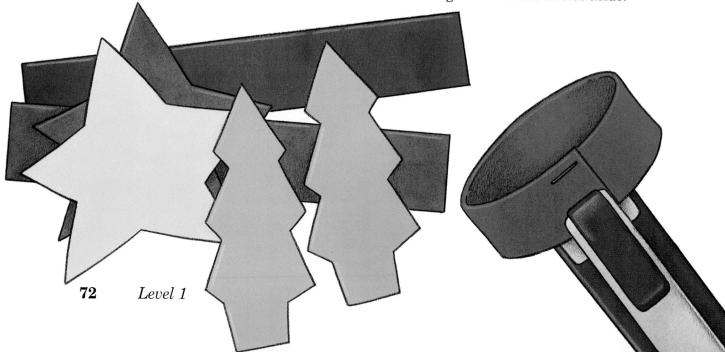

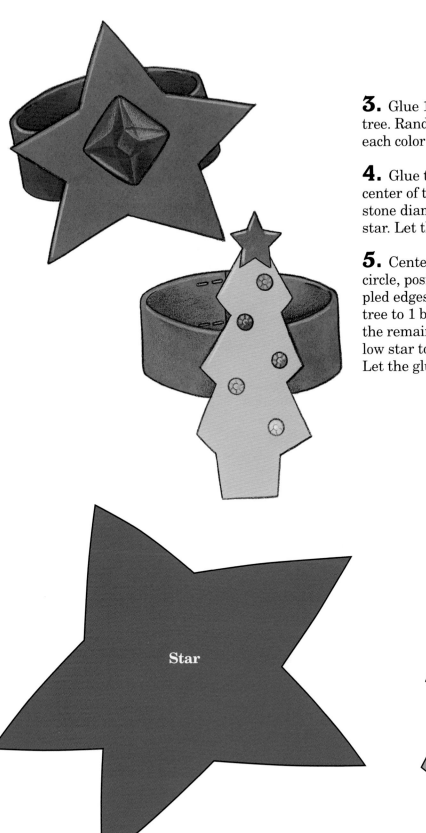

3. Glue 1 rhinestone star to the top of each tree. Randomly glue 1 rhinestone circle of each color on each tree. Let the glue dry.

4. Glue the red rhinestone diamond to the center of the blue star; glue the blue rhinestone diamond to the center of the yellow star. Let the glue dry.

5. Center and glue 1 tree on 1 red foam circle, positioning the tree opposite the stapled edges. Repeat to glue the remaining tree to 1 blue foam circle, the blue star to the remaining red foam circle, and the yellow star to the remaining blue foam circle. Let the glue dry.

Star

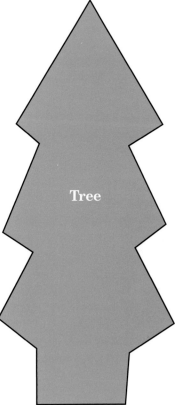

Tree

Paint Stick Ornaments

Stir up some fun with these ornaments! They are a great way to recycle old paint sticks.

You will need (for each ornament):
A grown-up
1 wooden paint stick
Silver webbing
Electric drill with small bit
Craft glue
Medium-tip permanent black marker
Scissors
1 (7-mm) red pom-pom
For Santa: 2 large wooden craft sticks (tongue depressor size); masking tape; red spray paint; 4 (½" x ¾") pieces and 1 (2½"-diameter) circle white, 2 (1¼") squares and 2 (¼" x 1⅛") pieces black, and 1 (4½"-diameter) circle red felt; 1 copper brad; 3 (6-mm) red and 3 (11-mm) silver sequins; stuffing; 2 blue wiggle eyes; 12" length red cording; 1 (15-mm) white pom-pom; small package decoration
For the reindeer: copper spray paint, 2 (1¼") squares black felt, 11½" length brown pipe cleaner, 2 brown wiggle eyes, 1 (25-mm) brown pom-pom, 1 small jingle bell, 15" length ¼"-wide red satin ribbon, 12" length silver cording

Note: Silver webbing is found in the spray paint section of stores. You'll find a metric conversion chart on page 5.

Santa
1. On 1 side only, cover 2½" of the shaped end of the paint stick with the masking tape. For each craft stick, tape off 1¼" of 1 end, putting tape on both sides of the stick. **Ask the grown-up** to watch as you spray-paint 1 side each of the paint stick and the craft sticks, using the red paint. Let the paint dry. Paint the remaining sides. Let the paint dry. Spray-paint each side of the

paint stick and the craft sticks with the silver webbing in the same manner. Let the webbing dry. Remove the tape.

2. **Ask the grown-up** to center and drill a hole in the unpainted end of the paint stick near the short edge. Then center and drill a second hole 2½" below the first hole. Center and drill a hole in the painted end of each craft stick near the short edge.

3. Glue 1 (½" x ¾") piece of white felt to each side of each craft stick where the red paint ends and the unpainted area begins (see the illustration). With the unpainted portion of the paint stick facedown, stack the craft sticks on top of the paint stick, aligning all of the holes. Slip the brad through the holes from beneath and bend the prongs. The side the arms are attached to is the back of the ornament.

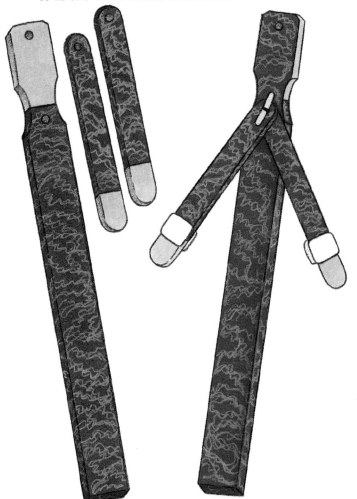

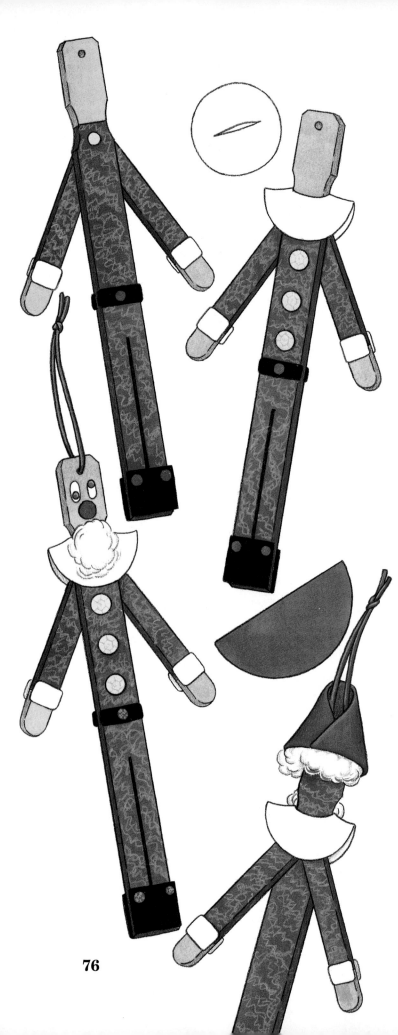

4. For the legs, using the marker and beginning 5¼" from the short painted end of the paint stick, draw a line along the center to the edge (see the illustration). For the boots, glue 1 (1¼") black felt square to each side of the painted end of the paint stick, aligning 1 edge of the square with the short end of the stick. For the belt, glue 1 (¼" x 1⅛") black felt piece to each side of the paint stick, 5" above the top of the boots. Glue 1 red sequin to the center front of the belt and to each top corner of the front of the boots. Let the glue dry.

5. For the collar, cut a slit in the center of the white felt circle. Slip the circle over the unpainted end of the paint stick and slide it to where the craft stick arms begin. Glue the collar in place. Center and glue the 3 silver sequins on the front of the ornament, spacing them evenly between the collar and the belt. Let the glue dry.

6. Referring to the illustration, for the beard, glue a small amount of stuffing to the center front of the collar. Center and glue the red pom-pom nose above the beard. Center and glue the wiggle eyes above the nose. For the hanger, thread the red cording through the hole in the top of the ornament. Align the ends and tie a knot in the cording below the ends. For the hair, glue a ring of stuffing around the end of the paint stick above the eyes. Let the glue dry.

7. Referring to the illustration, for the hat, cut the red circle in half. Using half of the circle, fold the piece around the top of the ornament, overlapping the ends and creating a cone shape. Make sure the hanger extends out of the opening at the top of the hat. Glue the overlapped ends in place. Glue the white pom-pom to the front top of the hat (see the photo). Glue the package to the front of 1 hand. Let the glue dry.

Reindeer

1. **Ask the grown-up** to watch as you spray-paint 1 side of the paint stick, using the copper paint. Let the paint dry. Paint the remaining side. Let the paint dry. Spray-paint each side of the paint stick with the silver webbing in the same manner. Let the webbing dry.

2. **Ask the grown-up** to center and drill a hole in 1 end of the paint stick near the short edge. Center and drill 2 holes side by side ½" below the first hole.

3. For the legs, using the marker and beginning 5¼" from the end without the holes, draw a line along the center of the paint stick to the edge (see the illustration). For the hoofs, glue 1 (1¼") black felt square to both sides of the bottom of the ornament, extending 1 edge of each felt square ¼" off the end of the stick. Cut a notch in the bottom center of the hoofs.

4. Referring to the illustration, for the antlers, cut 1 (6½") length and 2 (2½") lengths from the pipe cleaner. Fold the 6½" length into a U shape. Slip the ends through the 2 drilled holes from beneath; then bend the pipe cleaner prongs up. This is the front of the ornament. Wrap 1 (2½") length of pipe cleaner around each pipe cleaner prong.

5. Referring to the illustration, center and glue the wiggle eyes in place. Center and glue the brown pom-pom in place. Glue the red pom-pom in the center of the brown pom-pom. Thread the jingle bell onto the ribbon. Tie the ribbon into a bow around the ornament below the brown pom-pom.

6. For the hanger, thread the silver cording through the hole in the top of the ornament. Align the ends and tie a knot in the cording below the ends.

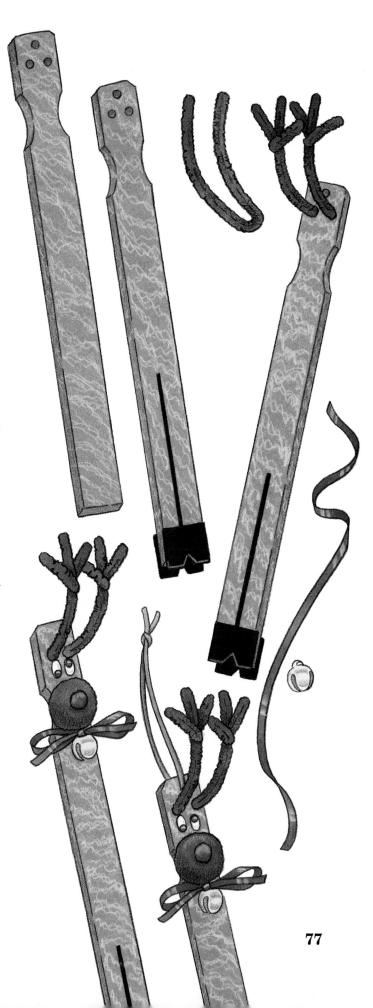

Tissue Paper Candles

Create colorful one-of-a-kind candles by decorating them with tissue paper and then dipping them in paraffin to seal in the design.

You will need:
A grown-up
Tissue paper: variety of colors, decorative print
Craft glue
3½" square gold foil (optional)
Embroidery scissors
Assorted pillar candles
2 boxes paraffin
1 empty coffee can
Medium-sized saucepan
Stove
Pliers

1. **For the mosaic candle,** tear the tissue paper into strips and small pieces or cut into the desired specific shapes to form a scene. Apply glue to 1 side of the tissue paper. Arrange the tissue paper on the candle and glue in place. Let the glue dry.

2. **For the foil snowflake candle,** fold the 3½" square of gold foil in half; fold in half again. Then fold in half on the diagonal. Using the embroidery scissors, cut notches out of the folded edges to form a snowflake. Unfold. Glue the snowflake to the outside of the candle. Let the glue dry.

3. **Ask the grown-up** to fill the saucepan with a small amount of water. Place the saucepan on the stove. Let the water simmer at a low heat. Place the paraffin in the can; place the can in the water. Let the paraffin melt. Using the pliers to hold each candle by its wick, quickly dip 1 candle at a time into the paraffin. For very tall candles, dip 1 end, allow the paraffin to cool and harden and then dip the other end.

Teatime Pin

This pin is sure to please anyone who collects teapots. And when making it, you will also be learning how to sculpt clay.

You will need:
A grown-up
Tracing paper
Pencil
Stick (approximately 15" long and ¼"
    in diameter)
Thick craft glue
2 (1½") lengths ½"-wide crocheted lace
Sculpey™ clay: 1 package each of 3
    different colors
Toothpick
Table knife
Oven
Baking sheet
Cement craft glue
Bar pin

Note: You'll find a metric conversion chart
on page 5.

1. Using the pencil, trace the teapot and
teacup patterns onto the tracing paper.
Do *not* cut them out. Set the patterns aside.

2. Break the stick into 2 (2") lengths and 3
(2¼") lengths. To make the shelves, place
the 2" sticks vertically on the work surface,
making sure the sticks are parallel and leaving approximately 1¾" between them. Apply
craft glue to the top end of each stick. Position 1 (2¼") stick horizontally across the vertical sticks and press the stick into the glue.
Repeat at the bottom end of the sticks. The
sticks will now look like a box. Apply glue to
the center of the 2 vertical sticks and glue
the remaining 2¼" stick in place. Let the
glue dry.

Turn the shelves over. Glue 1 length of
lace to the top stick, positioning the
straight edge of the lace along the middle of
the stick. Repeat to glue the remaining
length of lace along the middle stick. Let
the glue dry.

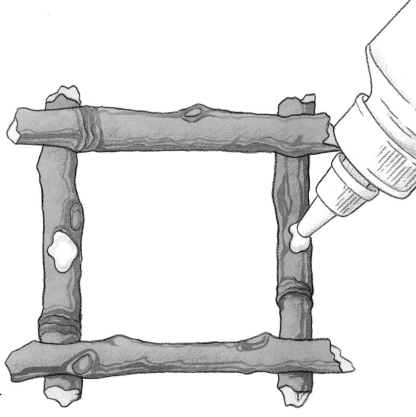

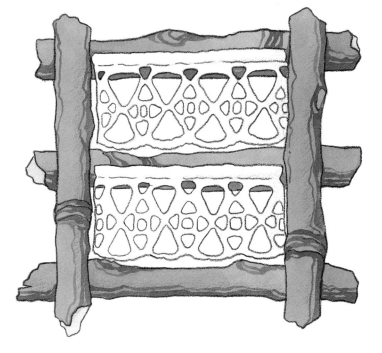

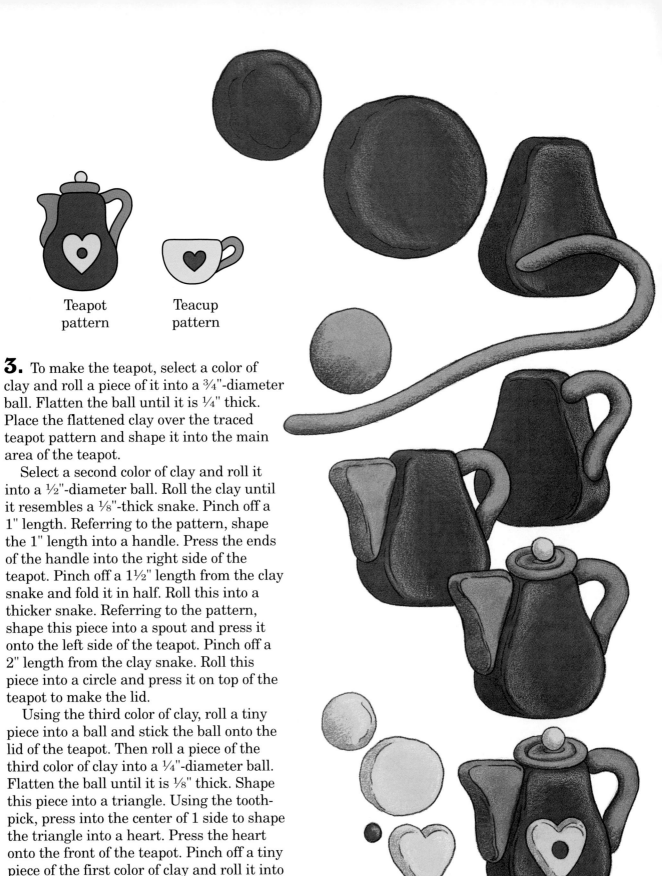

Teapot
pattern

Teacup
pattern

3. To make the teapot, select a color of clay and roll a piece of it into a ¾"-diameter ball. Flatten the ball until it is ¼" thick. Place the flattened clay over the traced teapot pattern and shape it into the main area of the teapot.

Select a second color of clay and roll it into a ½"-diameter ball. Roll the clay until it resembles a ⅛"-thick snake. Pinch off a 1" length. Referring to the pattern, shape the 1" length into a handle. Press the ends of the handle into the right side of the teapot. Pinch off a 1½" length from the clay snake and fold it in half. Roll this into a thicker snake. Referring to the pattern, shape this piece into a spout and press it onto the left side of the teapot. Pinch off a 2" length from the clay snake. Roll this piece into a circle and press it on top of the teapot to make the lid.

Using the third color of clay, roll a tiny piece into a ball and stick the ball onto the lid of the teapot. Then roll a piece of the third color of clay into a ¼"-diameter ball. Flatten the ball until it is ⅛" thick. Shape this piece into a triangle. Using the toothpick, press into the center of 1 side to shape the triangle into a heart. Press the heart onto the front of the teapot. Pinch off a tiny piece of the first color of clay and roll it into a ball. Press the ball into the center of the heart. Set the teapot aside.

4. To make the teacups, pinch off a piece of the second color of clay and roll it into a ½"-diameter ball. Flatten the ball into a circle that is ¼" thick. Using the table knife, cut the circle in half. Place the clay, 1 half at a time, over the traced teacup pattern and shape each into the main area of the teacup.

Pinch off 2 (¾") lengths from the remaining snake made from the second color in Step 3. Referring to the pattern, press 1 length onto each cup to form a handle. Pinch off 2 pieces from the first color of clay and roll each into a ⅜"-diameter ball. Flatten each ball until it is ⅛" thick. Shape these pieces into triangles. For each, using the toothpick, press into the center of 1 side to shape the triangle into a heart. Press 1 heart onto the front of each teacup.

5. Place the teapot and the teacups on the baking sheet. Following the manufacturer's instructions, **ask the grown-up** to bake them in the oven. Let them cool thoroughly.

6. Referring to the photo and using the craft glue, glue the teapot to the right side of the shelves, positioning the teapot so that the bottom touches the middle shelf and the top touches the top shelf. Glue the teacups at an angle on the bottom shelf. Let the glue dry.

7. Place the shelves facedown. Using the cement glue, glue the bar pin to the top shelf, holding it in place for several seconds. Let the glue dry.

Fantastic Frames

Whether you dream of being a race car driver or a movie star, these inexpensive frames will capture your imagination.

You will need (for each frame):
A grown-up
Tracing paper
Pencil
Scissors
Cardboard shirt box
Clear plastic report cover
Craft knife
Craft glue
Transparent tape
For the car: 5" x 8½" piece fabric, 27" length small rickrack, 2 (½"-diameter) round gems, 1 photo
For the sunglasses: silver spray paint, blue and pink strung beads, 19 (½"-diameter) round gems, 2 photos

Note: You'll find a metric conversion chart on page 5.

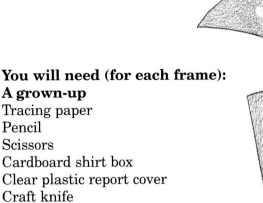

Car

1. Using the pencil, trace the car, frame stand, and window patterns on page 87 onto the tracing paper. Cut out the patterns. Transfer the car pattern and the markings 1 time and the frame stand pattern 2 times onto the shirt box. Transfer the window pattern onto the clear plastic. Cut out each piece along the outer edge. **Ask the grown-up** to use the craft knife to cut out the shaded window area of the car.

2. Apply glue to 1 side of the car. Place the fabric piece faceup on top of the glue. Let the glue dry. Trim the fabric that extends beyond the outline of the car. **Ask the grown-up** to use the craft knife to cut out the fabric from the window area of the car.

3. Glue the rickrack along the outer edge of the car and along the edge of the window opening, trimming to fit each edge. Glue 1 gem in place in the center of each wheel. Let the glue dry.

4. Fold each frame stand along the dotted line to form a tab. Apply glue to the outside of each tab. Glue 1 frame stand to the back of the car behind each wheel. Let the glue dry.

5. Apply glue to 1 side of the plastic window piece along the outer edge. Glue the plastic in place behind the window opening. Let the glue dry. Trim the photo to fit in the car window opening. Tape the photo in place.

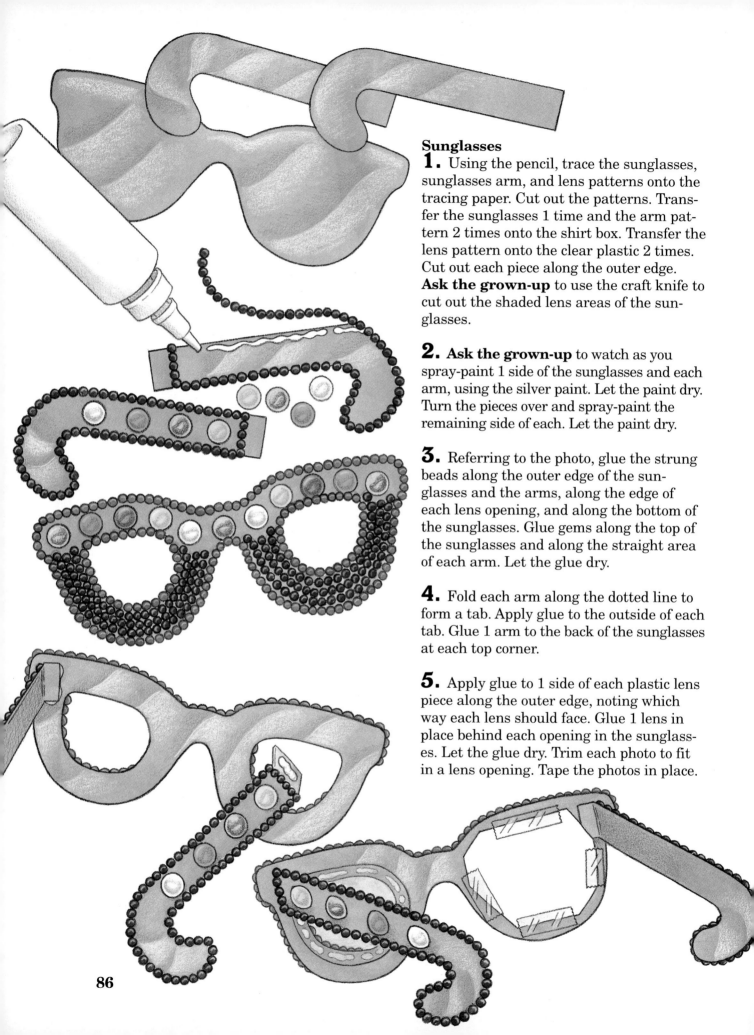

Sunglasses

1. Using the pencil, trace the sunglasses, sunglasses arm, and lens patterns onto the tracing paper. Cut out the patterns. Transfer the sunglasses 1 time and the arm pattern 2 times onto the shirt box. Transfer the lens pattern onto the clear plastic 2 times. Cut out each piece along the outer edge. **Ask the grown-up** to use the craft knife to cut out the shaded lens areas of the sunglasses.

2. Ask the grown-up to watch as you spray-paint 1 side of the sunglasses and each arm, using the silver paint. Let the paint dry. Turn the pieces over and spray-paint the remaining side of each. Let the paint dry.

3. Referring to the photo, glue the strung beads along the outer edge of the sunglasses and the arms, along the edge of each lens opening, and along the bottom of the sunglasses. Glue gems along the top of the sunglasses and along the straight area of each arm. Let the glue dry.

4. Fold each arm along the dotted line to form a tab. Apply glue to the outside of each tab. Glue 1 arm to the back of the sunglasses at each top corner.

5. Apply glue to 1 side of each plastic lens piece along the outer edge, noting which way each lens should face. Glue 1 lens in place behind each opening in the sunglasses. Let the glue dry. Trim each photo to fit in a lens opening. Tape the photos in place.

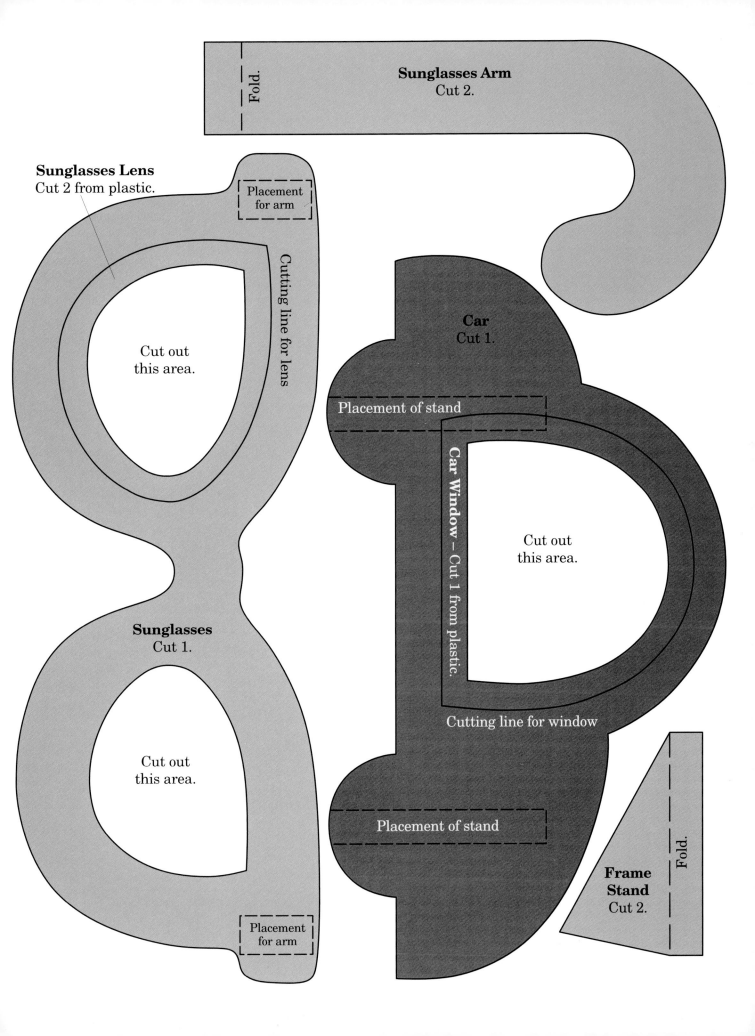

Sunglasses Arm
Cut 2.

Fold.

Sunglasses Lens
Cut 2 from plastic.

Placement
for arm

Cutting line for lens

Cut out
this area.

Car
Cut 1.

Placement of stand

Car Window – Cut 1 from plastic.

Cut out
this area.

Cutting line for window

Sunglasses
Cut 1.

Cut out
this area.

Placement of stand

Placement
for arm

Fold.

**Frame
Stand**
Cut 2.

Botanical Bookmarks

Gather small colorful flowers and ferns to create beautiful bookmarks. They make impressive gifts.

You will need:
Waxed paper
Heavy books
Assorted flowers and ferns
White paper
Ruler
Clear peel-and-stick vinyl shelf covering
Colored paper
Craft glue
Scissors
Pinking shears
Hole punch
Raffia

Note: You'll find a metric conversion chart on page 5.

1. Place 2 sheets of waxed paper between the pages of a heavy book. Slip the flowers and the ferns between the sheets of waxed paper and shut the book. Place more books on top of this book. Press the foliage for several days.

2. For the bookmark without a colored paper background, arrange the flowers and the ferns as desired on a sheet of white paper. Measure the height and the width of the arrangement. Cut a piece of vinyl shelf covering equal to the height plus 2" by twice the width plus 2".

3. Fold the vinyl in half, with the paper sides together. Unfold the vinyl. Peel the paper backing from the right half. Carefully position the flowers and the ferns on the sticky side. Replace the paper backing over the flowers and the ferns and rub gently with your fingers to flatten.

4. Peel away the paper backing. Fold the vinyl in half again to seal in the flowers and the ferns, smoothing the vinyl as you work.

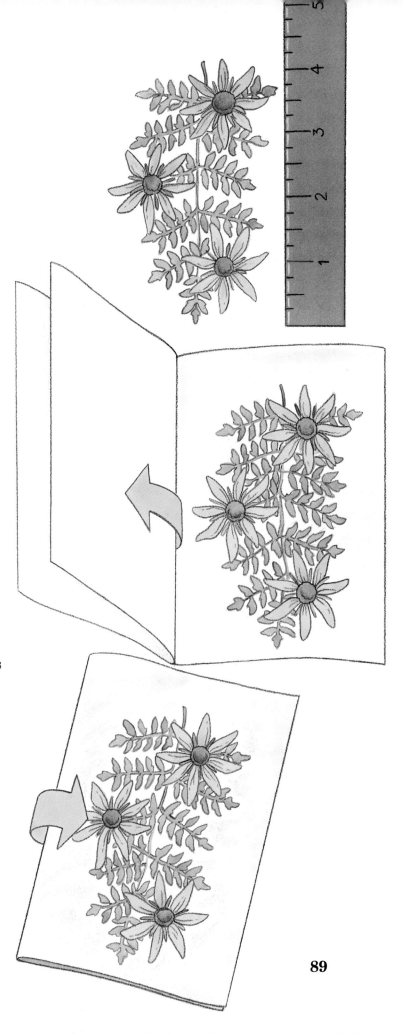

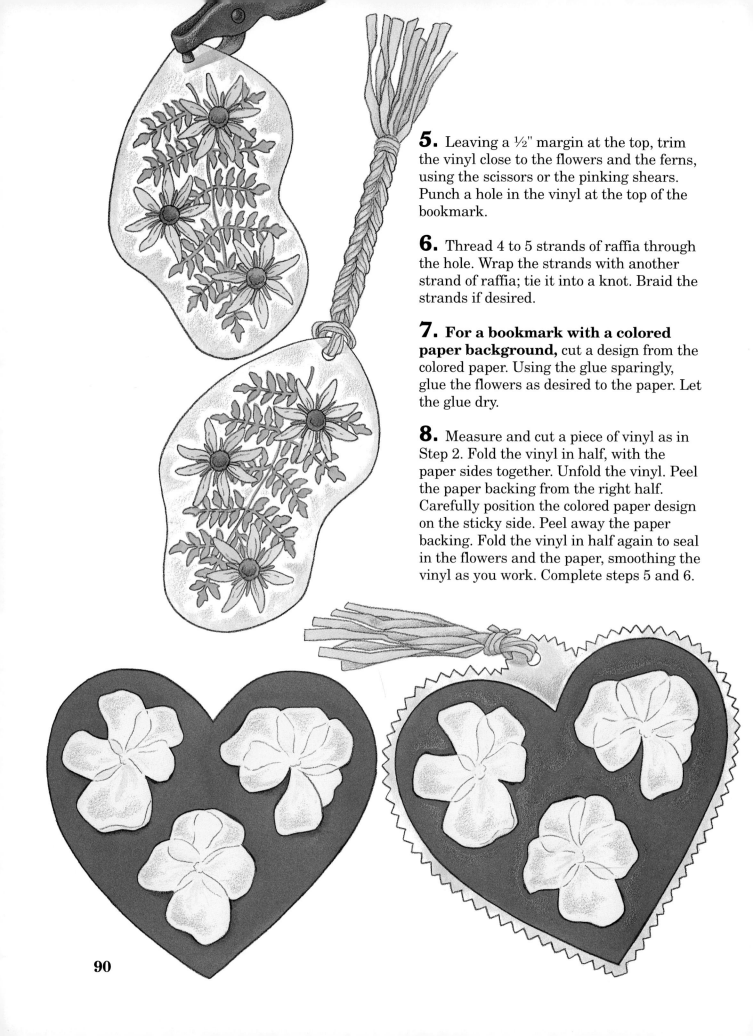

5. Leaving a ½" margin at the top, trim the vinyl close to the flowers and the ferns, using the scissors or the pinking shears. Punch a hole in the vinyl at the top of the bookmark.

6. Thread 4 to 5 strands of raffia through the hole. Wrap the strands with another strand of raffia; tie it into a knot. Braid the strands if desired.

7. For a bookmark with a colored paper background, cut a design from the colored paper. Using the glue sparingly, glue the flowers as desired to the paper. Let the glue dry.

8. Measure and cut a piece of vinyl as in Step 2. Fold the vinyl in half, with the paper sides together. Unfold the vinyl. Peel the paper backing from the right half. Carefully position the colored paper design on the sticky side. Peel away the paper backing. Fold the vinyl in half again to seal in the flowers and the paper, smoothing the vinyl as you work. Complete steps 5 and 6.

90

Permanent Prints

Leave your mark with one of these decorative molds. They are a gift that is sure to be a hands down favorite.

You will need:
A grown-up
Oven
2 cups all-purpose flour
½ cup salt
Medium-sized bowl
Water
Foil
Rolling pin
Toothpick
Drinking straw
Gold acrylic paint
Clear acrylic varnish
Medium paintbrush
Red paint pen
2 (22") lengths 1½"-wide ribbon

Note: You'll find a metric conversion chart on page 5.

1. **Ask the grown-up** to preheat the oven to 250°.

2. Mix the flour and the salt in the bowl. Slowly add a little water. Using your hands, shape the mixture into a soft dough ball, adding more water as necessary. Divide the ball in half. Roll out each half on a floured piece of foil. Flour the top of each dough piece. Press your hand into 1 piece and your foot into the other.

3. With the toothpick, cut around the prints, leaving a border around the edges (see the photo). Using the straw, make a hole in each top corner, ½" from the side edge.

4. **Ask the grown-up** to bake the prints for 2 hours. Then turn the prints over and bake them for 1 more hour. Let them cool.

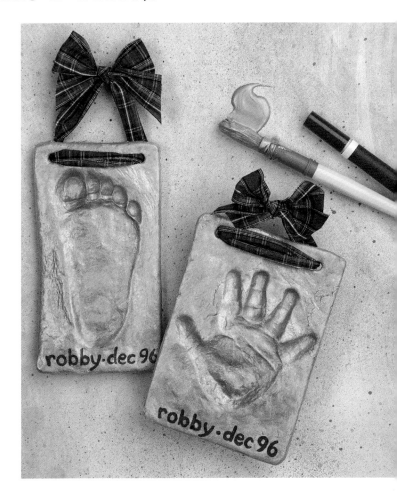

5. Dust off the excess flour on both sides. **Ask the grown-up** to mix 1 part gold paint and 2 parts varnish. With the paintbrush, paint 1 side of each print. Let the paint dry. Repeat to paint the opposite sides.

6. Using the red paint pen, write your name and the date across the bottom of each print. Let the paint dry.

7. Referring to the photo, thread 1 ribbon length through each pair of holes. Tie the ends of each length into a bow.

Cutwork Pillowcases

Transform plain pillowcases into lively linens by cutting shapes in the open end. Colorful fabric paint seals the cut edges.

You will need (for each pillowcase):
Tracing paper
Pencil
Scissors
Purchased solid-colored pillowcase
Waxed paper

For the fish pillowcase: green, blue, yellow, red, and white dimensional fabric paints
For the heart pillowcase: pink dimensional fabric paint, 1⅓ yards ¼"-wide blue satin ribbon, washable glue

Note: To make the cutout designs stand out, we put a striped pillowcase on each pillow before slipping on the decorated pillowcase. You'll find a metric conversion chart on page 5.

1. Using the pencil, trace the desired pattern on the tracing paper. Cut out the pattern. Referring to the photo, transfer the pattern onto 1 layer of the pillowcase at the open end. Cut out the fabric from inside each shape.

2. Slide a piece of waxed paper under the shapes and between the layers of the pillow-case. Referring to the photo, outline the shapes with the dimensional paints.

3. For the fish pillowcase, using the white paint, paint circles above each fish's mouth for bubbles.

4. For each, let the paint dry for 6 hours. Remove the waxed paper. Reline the pillowcase with a new piece of waxed paper. Let the paint dry overnight. (Wait at least 72 hours before washing.)

5. For the heart pillowcase, cut the ribbon into 4 equal lengths. Tie each length into a bow. Glue each bow in place.

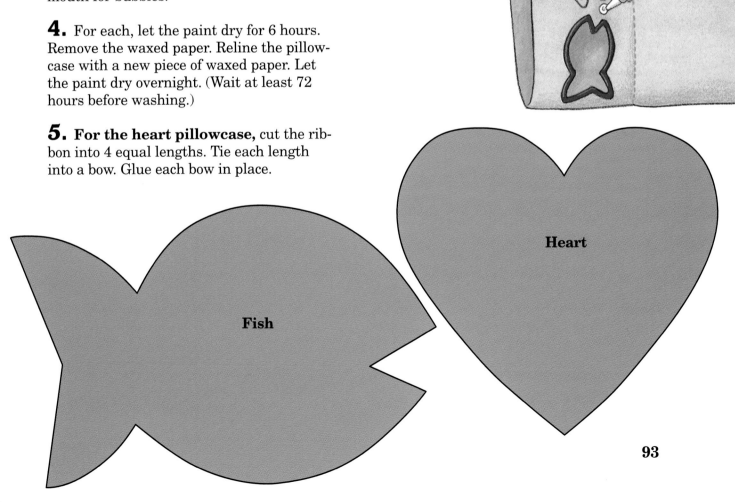

Fish

Heart

93

Dip and Drip Flowerpots

Give plain pots a colorful personality. Just dunk the rims and let the paint run! These bright containers are perfect for planting a windowsill herb garden or adding pizzazz to a simple green plant.

You will need:
Newspaper
Latex paints in desired colors
Foil baking pans (1 for each color of paint)
Assorted clay flowerpots

1. Cover the work surface with the newspaper. Pour the paints into separate foil pans. The paint should be ¼" to ½" deep in each pan.

2. For the single-color pot, turn the pot upside down and dip the rim into 1 color of paint. (The deeper you dip the pot, the wider the band of color will be.) Turn the pot right side up and let the paint run down the sides. (If the paint does not drip as much as you desire, mix a little water into the paint and redip the pot.) Let the paint dry.

3. For the multicolored pot, complete Step 2. When the paint is dry, dip the pot into a different color of paint, making sure not to dip as much of the rim into the paint as the first time or the second layer of paint will cover the first layer. Let the paint dry. If desired, dip the pot a third time, making sure not to dip as much of the rim as the second time. Let the paint dry.

4. For the marbleized rim pot, swirl 1 color of paint into a pan containing a different color of paint. Dip the rim of the pot into the pan so that it touches both colors of paint. Twist the pot to swirl the colors together on the rim. Turn the pot right side up and let the paint run down the sides. Let the paint dry.

5. Put any plant of your choice in the pot.

95

Sea Sculptures

These mystical creatures from the deep will look as if they are floating through the branches when hung on your tree. After the holidays, transform them into a mobile by tying them to a coat hanger.

You will need (for each creature):
A grown-up
Tracing paper
Pencil
Scissors
Medium-tip permanent black marker
Newspaper
Small utility kitchen knife
Plastic knife
White tissue paper
Liquid starch
Plastic cup
Paintbrush
Long thin needle
Gold metallic thread
For the fish: 10" x 5" x 1½" piece
   Styrofoam; 2 pushpins; 35 round tooth-
   picks; craft glue; orange, black, and white
   acrylic paints
For the sea horse: 6" x 9" x 1" piece
   Styrofoam; 26 round toothpicks; craft
   glue; light blue, golden yellow, light
   green, white, copper, and black acrylic
   paints; sponge; 4 Styrofoam plates
For the starfish: 9" x 10" x 1½" piece
   Styrofoam; fuchsia, orange, and white
   acrylic paints; sponge; 2 Styrofoam plates

Note: This project should be made by older
children. The fish and the sea horse have
edges that must be handled with care. You'll
find a metric conversion chart on page 5.

Fish
1. Using the pencil, trace the fish pattern
on page 101 onto the tracing paper. Cut out
the pattern. Using the marker, transfer the
pattern to the Styrofoam block. Cover the
work surface with newspaper. **Ask the
grown-up** to cut out the fish, using the
kitchen knife and holding the blade vertically. (If a section breaks off, glue it back in
place; then reinforce the area by imbedding a
toothpick in the Styrofoam. Let the glue dry.)

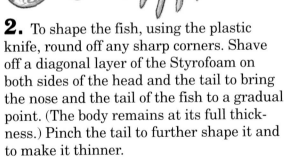

2. To shape the fish, using the plastic
knife, round off any sharp corners. Shave
off a diagonal layer of the Styrofoam on
both sides of the head and the tail to bring
the nose and the tail of the fish to a gradual
point. (The body remains at its full thickness.) Pinch the tail to further shape it and
to make it thinner.

3. For the top, bottom, and side fins,
referring to the pattern, insert toothpicks
into the fish. (Be sure to make side fins on
both sides of the fish.) For areas where only
a little of the toothpick is needed, you can
break a toothpick in half. Dip the broken
end into the glue and insert the piece into
the fish. For the eyes, insert 1 pushpin into
each side of the fish where indicated.

4. Tear the tissue paper into 1" to 2" pieces. Pour the liquid starch into the cup. Dip the tissue paper pieces into the liquid starch. Cover the entire fish, including the fins and the eyes, with the tissue paper, overlapping the pieces. Apply a second and third layer of dry tissue paper pieces over the first wet layer. Smooth these new layers with a finger that has been dipped in the starch. Let the fish dry for 24 hours.

5. Referring to the photo, paint the fish, using the white, orange, and black paints and letting the paint dry between colors. Mix equal parts of the white and the orange to make the peach. Then paint the outer ring of the eyes and the inside of the mouth. Let the paint dry. For the hanger, thread the needle with a 16" length of gold thread. Stick the needle through the fish body below the top fin. With the cut ends aligned, tie a knot 1" from the ends.

Sea Horse
1. Using the pencil, trace the solid line and the broken lines of the pattern on page 101 onto the tracing paper. Cut out the sea horse along the *solid* line. Using the marker, transfer the pattern and the markings to the Styrofoam block. Referring to Step 1 on page 97, **ask the grown-up** to cut out the sea horse.

2. Using the plastic knife, carve out the areas indicated on the pattern with broken lines. Shave off a diagonal layer of Styrofoam on both sides of the rounded end of the tail. Pinch the end of the tail to further shape it and to make it thinner.

3. To make the spikes, break 20 toothpicks in half. Working with 1 at a time, dip the broken end of each half into the glue; insert 1 toothpick piece into each point on both sides of the sea horse (see the pattern). To make the back fin, insert the 6 remaining toothpicks into the sea horse as indicated.

4. Referring to Step 4 on page 98, cover the sea horse, including the back fin, with tissue paper pieces dipped in the liquid starch. Do *not* cover the toothpick spikes. Let the sea horse dry for 24 hours.

5. Using the light blue paint and the paintbrush, paint the entire sea horse. Let the paint dry. Pour a blob of golden yellow paint onto 1 Styrofoam plate. Wet the sponge and squeeze out the excess water. Dip the sponge into the golden yellow and paint the bowed out area of the sea horse stomach. Rinse the sponge and squeeze out the excess water. Pour a blob each of the light green, white, and copper paints onto separate Styrofoam plates. Randomly tear small pieces out of the sponge. Dip the sponge into the light green and then into the white. Referring to the photo, lightly sponge-paint 1 side of the head, the side, and the tip of the fin. Let the paint dry. Repeat on the opposite side. Rinse the sponge and squeeze out the excess water. Dip the sponge into the copper. Very lightly sponge-paint over the green and the white with the copper.

6. Referring to the photo, on 1 side, use the copper paint and the paintbrush, to paint lines across the width of the sea horse at each point, beginning at the base of the neck; paint the eye and each of the toothpick spikes. Let the paint dry. Repeat on the opposite side.

Using the black paint and the paintbrush, paint a ring around the copper eye on 1 side; paint lines across the width of the sea horse at each point; and paint a line along the edge of the stomach and along the inside edge of the tail. Let the paint dry. Repeat on the opposite side. Using the white paint and

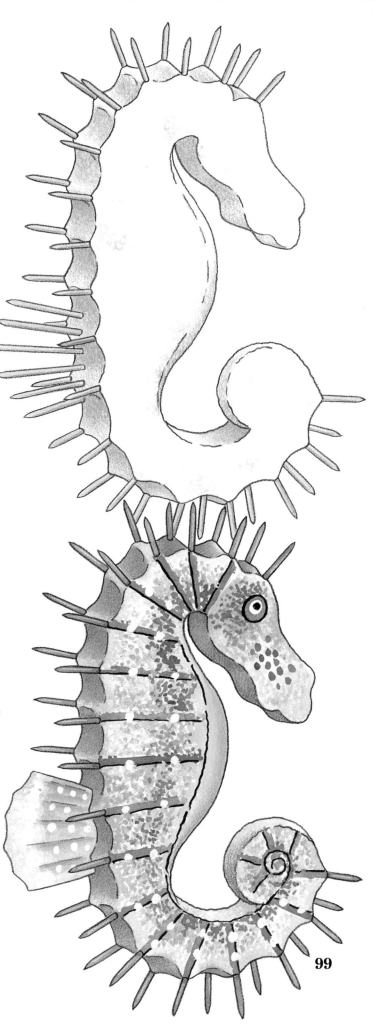

7. For the hanger, thread the needle with a 16" length of gold thread. Stick the needle through the sea horse at the top of the neck. With the cut ends aligned, tie a knot 1" from the ends.

Starfish
1. Referring to Step 1 on page 98, trace and transfer the pattern and the markings on page 102. **Ask the grown-up** to cut out the starfish. Using the plastic knife, shave off a diagonal layer of the Styrofoam along both edges of each arm of the starfish, beginning at the broken line on the pattern. Referring to Step 4 on page 98, cover the starfish with tissue paper pieces dipped in the liquid starch. Let the starfish dry for 24 hours.

2. Using the paintbrush, paint the entire starfish with the fuchsia paint. Let the paint dry. Pour a blob each of the orange and white paints onto separate Styrofoam plates. Randomly tear small pieces out of the sponge. Wet the sponge and squeeze out the excess water. Dip the sponge into the orange and then into the white. Referring to the photo, lightly sponge-paint the top of the starfish. Let the paint dry. Rinse the sponge and squeeze out the excess water. Dip the sponge into the orange. Lightly sponge-paint over the mixed orange and white. Let the paint dry. Then sponge-paint the bottom of the starfish. Let the paint dry. Rinse the sponge and squeeze out the excess water. Dip the sponge into the white. Sponge-paint along the top ridge of each arm of the starfish. Using the white paint and the paintbrush, paint rows of dots along each arm. Let the paint dry.

the paintbrush, paint a white area inside 1 eye; paint polka dots on the body and the fin. Let the paint dry. Paint a black dot inside the center of the eye. Let the paint dry. Repeat on the opposite side.

3. For the hanger, thread the needle with a 16" length of gold thread. Stick the needle through 1 arm of the starfish. With the cut ends aligned, tie a knot 1" from the ends.

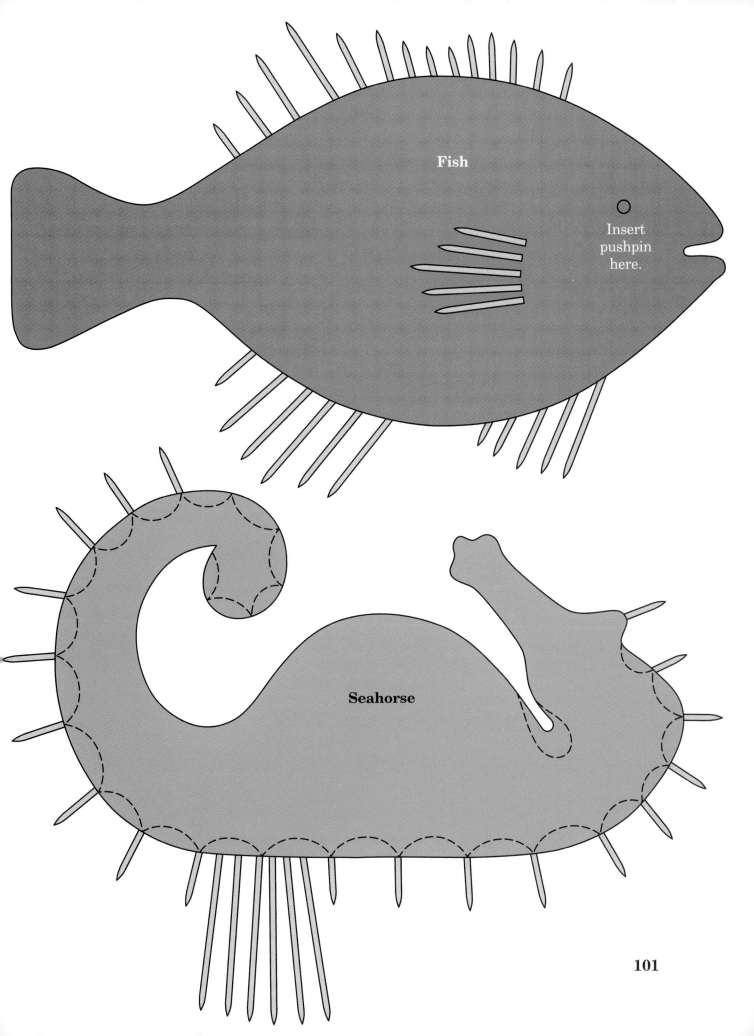

Fish

Insert
pushpin
here.

Seahorse

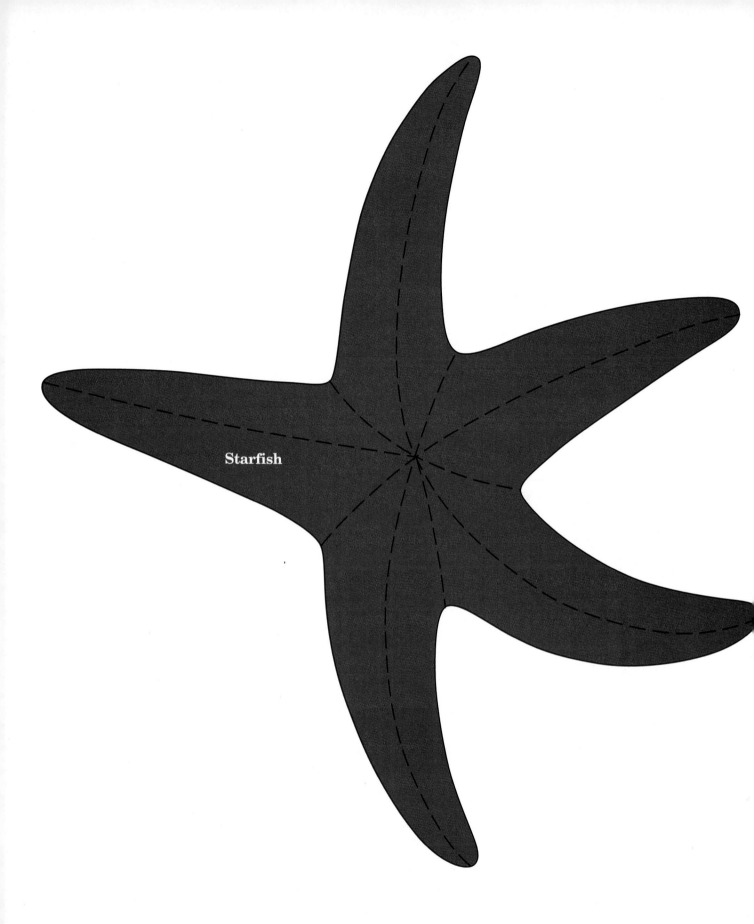

Starfish

Desk Set

Many of the materials for this nature-lover's desk set can be found in the old shoe box that holds your collections. When assembling the paperweight and the pencil holder, using the correct glue is the key to success.

You will need (for the paperweight):
Waxed paper
Assorted polished rocks
Silicone adhesive
1 (3"-diameter) Styrofoam ball
Tile grout
Paper towels
Clear acrylic spray sealer

Note: You'll find a metric conversion chart on page 5.

1. Cover the work surface with the waxed paper. Using the silicone adhesive, glue the rocks onto the Styrofoam ball as desired. Let the adhesive dry.

2. Use your fingers to spread the tile grout between the rocks, pressing and smoothing the grout into the cracks. Let the grout dry approximately 10 minutes.

3. Using damp paper towels, clean the excess grout from the rocks. Be careful not to loosen the grout from the ball or from in between the cracks. Let the grout dry.

4. Lightly spray the ball with 1 coat of acrylic sealer. Let the sealer dry.

You will need (for the pencil holder):
1 powdered drink canister
Wooden craft stick
Thick craft glue
Spanish moss
Assorted rubber bugs

1. Peel the label off the canister. Using the craft stick, spread the glue around the outside of the canister and 1" inside the top. Press the Spanish moss onto the glued portions. Let the glue dry.

2. Glue the bugs onto the moss. Let the glue dry.

Funky Flowers for Your Feet

Tie-dyed socks are a cool present by themselves, but when packaged to resemble a pot of tulips, they're a gift that really blossoms!

You will need (for 4 flowers):
A grown-up
3 medium-sized plastic bowls
Nontoxic fabric dye: kelly green, fuchsia,
    purple
4 pairs thin cotton socks
Rubber bands
Tongs
Old towel
Ruler
2 (36") lengths ¼"-diameter dowels
Saw
4 facial tissues
Transparent tape
Disappearing-ink fabric marker
Knife
1 (4"-diameter) Styrofoam ball
4"-diameter clay pot
Craft glue
Shredded yellow paper

Note: You'll find a metric conversion chart
on page 5.

1. **Ask the grown-up** to pour hot water
into each plastic bowl. Following the manufacturer's directions, dissolve each color of
dye in a separate plastic bowl. Wet the
socks in warm water.

2. Wrap rubber bands around 4 socks as
desired. Submerge 1 pair in the fuchsia dye
and 1 pair in the purple dye.

3. For the remaining 2 pairs, roll up each
sock from the toe to the heel. Wrap 1 rubber
band around the center of the roll. Wrap 2
rubber bands around the cuff. Submerge
both pairs of socks in the green dye.

4. Let all the socks soak for 10 to 20 minutes, stirring them occasionally with the
tongs. Remove the socks from the dye, 1 at a
time, using the tongs. Run each sock under
cold water until the water runs clear. Take

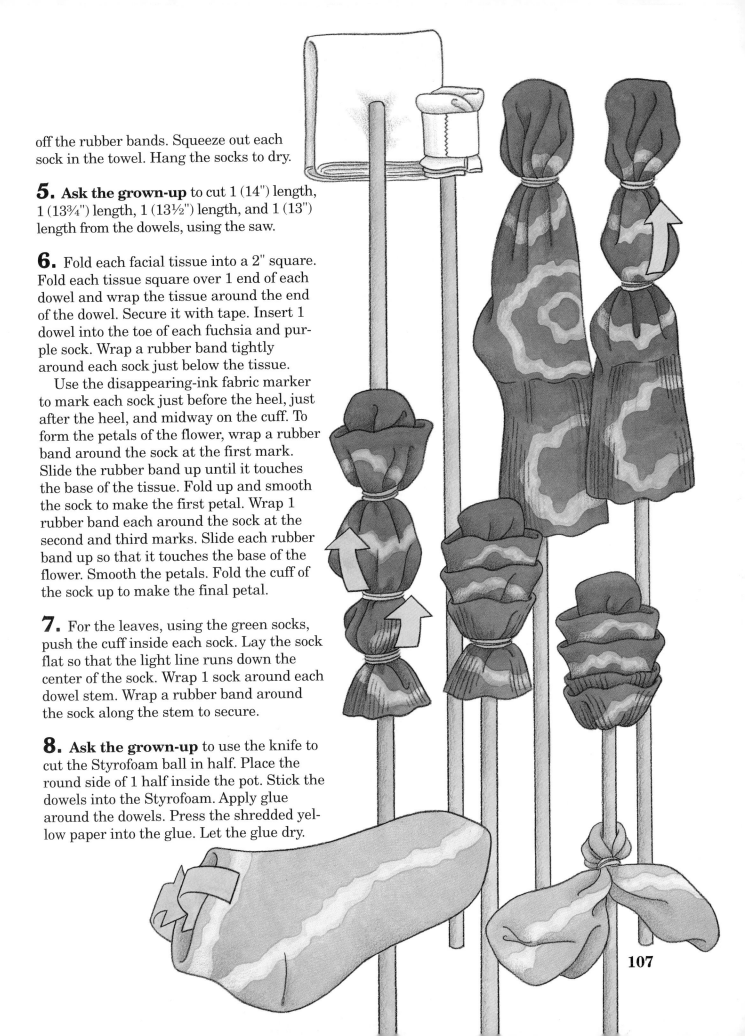

off the rubber bands. Squeeze out each sock in the towel. Hang the socks to dry.

5. **Ask the grown-up** to cut 1 (14") length, 1 (13¾") length, 1 (13½") length, and 1 (13") length from the dowels, using the saw.

6. Fold each facial tissue into a 2" square. Fold each tissue square over 1 end of each dowel and wrap the tissue around the end of the dowel. Secure it with tape. Insert 1 dowel into the toe of each fuchsia and purple sock. Wrap a rubber band tightly around each sock just below the tissue.

Use the disappearing-ink fabric marker to mark each sock just before the heel, just after the heel, and midway on the cuff. To form the petals of the flower, wrap a rubber band around the sock at the first mark. Slide the rubber band up until it touches the base of the tissue. Fold up and smooth the sock to make the first petal. Wrap 1 rubber band each around the sock at the second and third marks. Slide each rubber band up so that it touches the base of the flower. Smooth the petals. Fold the cuff of the sock up to make the final petal.

7. For the leaves, using the green socks, push the cuff inside each sock. Lay the sock flat so that the light line runs down the center of the sock. Wrap 1 sock around each dowel stem. Wrap a rubber band around the sock along the stem to secure.

8. **Ask the grown-up** to use the knife to cut the Styrofoam ball in half. Place the round side of 1 half inside the pot. Stick the dowels into the Styrofoam. Apply glue around the dowels. Press the shredded yellow paper into the glue. Let the glue dry.

Collectible Keepers

Whether you want to organize all of your earrings and favorite baubles or store your miniature cars, these boxes are the answer.

You will need (for each box):
Clear plastic tackle box
Craft glue
Paintbrush
For the jewelry box: assortment of
    colored tissue paper, decoupage coating,
    assortment of plastic rhinestones
For the car box: black acrylic paint, map,
    scissors, yellow paint pen, small plastic
    cars

Jewelry Box
1. Tear the tissue paper into small pieces.
Cover a quarter of the box lid with the
craft glue. Stick the tissue onto the glue.
Continue in this manner until the entire
lid is covered. Let the glue dry.

2. Coat the lid with the decoupage coating. Let the coating dry.

3. Glue the rhinestones onto the box as
desired. Let the glue dry.

Car Box
1. Paint the outside edge of the box lid
with the black paint. Let the paint dry.

2. Cut a portion of the map to fit inside
the painted border. Glue the map to the
box. Let the glue dry.

3. Using the yellow paint pen, paint
the broken line onto the black border (see
the photo). Let the paint dry. Glue cars
onto the painted road as desired. Let
the glue dry.

Parents' Workshop

Great Gifts
for Children

Reindeer Tie

Your little "deer" will love his junior holiday version of a big-boy tie. And you'll love the elastic band that makes it easy to put on and requires no tying.

You will need:
Pencil
Tracing paper
Scissors
Disappearing-ink fabric marker
¼ yard red check cotton fabric

6" x 11" piece fusible interfacing
Brown wool scraps
Iron and ironing board
6" x 11" piece paper-backed fusible web
Tan felt scraps
Continued on next page

112

Straight pins
Sewing machine
Thread: dark brown, white, red
Dark brown embroidery floss
Needles: embroidery, hand sewing
11" length ¼"-wide elastic
1 (¾") brown wooden button
11" length ⅜"-wide red satin ribbon
⅜"-diameter jingle bell
Silk floral holly sprig
Fabric paints: black in a tube, red brush-on
½"-wide flat paintbrush

Note: All seams are ¼". You'll find a metric conversion chart on page 5.

1. Using the pencil, transfer the tie and ear patterns on page 114 onto the tracing paper. Cut them out. Using the disappearing-ink fabric marker, transfer the tie pattern to the red check fabric 2 times and to the fusible interfacing 1 time. Cut out the tie pieces. Transfer the ear to the wool 2 times. Cut out the ears. Following the manufacturer's instructions, fuse the interfacing tie piece to the wrong side of 1 red check tie piece. This is the front tie piece.

2. Lay the paper-backed fusible web on top of the antlers and head patterns on page 114. Using the pencil, trace each piece. Cut the pieces apart, leaving a generous margin around each piece. Following the manufacturer's instructions, fuse the head to the wrong side of the brown wool and the antlers to the wrong side of the tan felt. Cut out each piece along the traced lines. Remove the paper backing. Referring to the photo for placement, pin the head on the right side of the front tie piece. Tuck the straight end of each antler under the top of the head piece; pin them in place. Tuck the ears under the head piece, just below the antlers; pin them in place. Fuse the pieces in place.

3. Set the sewing machine for a medium-width zigzag. Using dark brown thread, satin-stitch around the head, beginning at the top. Using 3 strands of the embroidery floss, blanket-stitch by hand around the edges of the antlers.

4. With the right sides facing and the raw edges aligned, pin the tie pieces together. Set the sewing machine for a small straight stitch. Using the white thread, stitch around the edges of the tie, leaving open where indicated on the pattern. Set the machine for a medium-width loose zigzag and stitch around the edges just stitched to reinforce them. Turn the tie right side out, using the eraser of the pencil to push out the corners. Press the tie. Turn ¼" of the raw edges of the opening to the inside and press. Slipstitch the opening closed. Fold the top of the tie along the fold line and pin it to the front of the tie. Slip ⅜" of each cut end of the elastic between the layers of the top fold; pin the ends in place. Using a blindstitch and the white thread, tack the folded area of the tie to the main area of the tie, catching the elastic in the stitching.

5. Using the disappearing-ink fabric marker, transfer the face details to the head. Using the brown thread, sew the button nose in place. Tie the satin ribbon into a bow and trim the ends. Using the red thread, tack the bow in place just below the head; then tack the jingle bell in place just below the bow. Tack the holly sprig in place on top of the head between the antlers.

6. Referring to the photo and using the black fabric paint, paint the eyebrows, the eyes, and the mouth. Using the red fabric paint and the paintbrush, lightly paint the cheeks and inside the reindeer's ears. Let the paint dry.

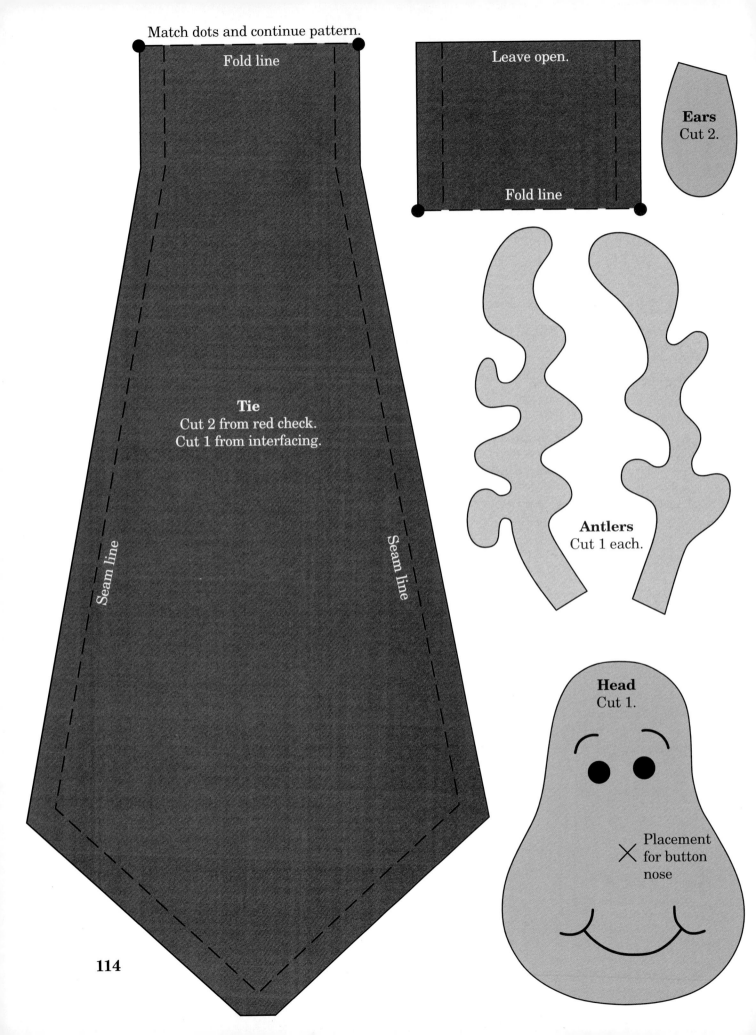

Match dots and continue pattern.

Fold line

Tie
Cut 2 from red check.
Cut 1 from interfacing.

Seam line

Seam line

Fold line

114

Leave open.

Fold line

Ears
Cut 2.

Antlers
Cut 1 each.

Head
Cut 1.

✕ Placement
for button
nose

Angel Sweatshirt

You can make this heavenly shirt in the flap of an angel's wings. Don't let the painted design intimidate you. Only the most basic painting skills are required here.

You will need:

Iron-on transfer pen
Sheet of plain white paper
Purchased plain white sweatshirt
Iron and ironing board
Ruler
Fabric paints: flesh color, hair color, darker
    shade of hair color, gold glitter, red
Paintbrushes
Scissors
6½" length lace
Needle
White thread
20" length 1½"-wide white sheer ribbon
12" length ⅛"-wide gold ribbon
Medium-point gold fabric paint pen
2 size-30 green rhinestones and backs
Safety pin

Note: You'll find a metric conversion chart
on page 5.

1. Using the transfer pen, transfer the
angel pattern to the paper. Position the
pattern on the center front of the sweatshirt so that the top of the halo is approximately 2" below the neckline. Lightly iron
to transfer the pattern.

2. Center the sheet of paper inside the
sweatshirt and underneath the pattern.
Paint the face and the hands with the flesh
color. Let the paint dry.

3. Cut scallops along 1 long edge of the
lace. Using the needle and the thread,
gather the edge opposite the scallops to
measure 1½". Tack to secure. Tie the
sheer ribbon into a bow. Tie the gold
ribbon around the center knot of the
sheer bow. Tack the bow to the gathered
end of the lace.

4. Paint the hair, using the hair color. Let
the paint dry. Outline the hair curls with
the darker shade of the hair color. Using
the gold paint pen, outline the halo, the
dress, the wings, and the feet. Let the paint
dry. Fill in the feet with gold. Paint over the
halo with gold glitter paint. Paint the
mouth with red. Let the paint dry. Heat-set
the paint, following the manufacturer's
instructions.

5. Referring to the photo for placement,
set the rhinestone eyes by pushing the tabs
of each through to the wrong side. Using
the tip of a blunt pair of scissors, press the
tabs towards the center of each rhinestone.
Using the small safety pin, pin the lace
dress in place. Before laundering, remove
the lace dress.

Halo
Place above
hair.

Eye
placement

Angel

Fancy Gloves and Headbands

Add some brightly colored beads to plain purchased gloves and headbands for a flashy fashion statement.

You will need:
Elastic thread
Needle
Purchased knit gloves
Purchased knit headbands
Assorted wooden or plastic beads

1. Thread the needle with the elastic thread and triple-knot 1 end. Take several small stitches on the inside of the top of the glove cuff or the headband to secure the thread. Push the needle through to the outside of the glove or the headband.

2. For individual beads, thread 1 bead onto the elastic. Push the needle through the glove cuff or the headband and take several small stitches on the wrong side to secure. Trim the elastic close to the last stitch. Continue adding beads as desired.

3. For row of beads, thread 1 bead onto the elastic. Push the needle through the glove cuff or the headband and take 1 small stitch on the wrong side. Push the needle back to the right side, close to the bead just attached; add 1 bead. Push the needle to the wrong side and take 1 small stitch. Continue adding beads in this manner until the row is the desired length. Take several small stitches on the wrong side to secure. Trim the elastic close to the last stitch.

Sweet Dreams Sleepwear

Visions of sugarplums will dance in her head when she slumbers in this lollipop ensemble made by embellishing an oversize T-shirt.

You will need:
Purchased plain white T-shirt in size larger
  than usually worn
Ruler
Disappearing-ink fabric marker
Scissors
2 yards 2"-wide eyelet for sleeves and
  shirt hem
Liquid ravel preventer
Sewing machine
White thread
Iron and ironing board
Sheet of paper
Bowls and cups in various sizes to make
  lollipop circles
Fine-grade sandpaper
Fabric paint pens: gray, 5 different colors to
  match boxer shorts fabric
Iridescent glitter paint
Paintbrushes
24" length each ¼"-wide satin ribbon in 5
  different colors to match boxer shorts
  fabric
Needle
5 small safety pins (optional)
Purchased boxer shorts pattern
Fabric for boxer shorts
Elastic for waistband of boxer shorts

Note: Designated amount of eyelet will
edge an adult-sized small T-shirt. Adjust
the amount of eyelet purchased if making a
larger or smaller T-shirt. You'll find a
metric conversion chart on page 5.

1. Determine the desired length of the T-
shirt. Using the ruler and disappearing-
ink fabric marker, measure and mark the
T-shirt at this length. Cut the T-shirt along
the marked line. Cut the band off each
sleeve. Cut 2 (17") lengths and 1 (38")
length of eyelet. Apply liquid ravel
preventer to each cut end. With the right
sides facing and the edges aligned, zigzag 1

(17") length of eyelet to each sleeve,
overlapping the cut ends. With the right
sides facing and the edges aligned, zigzag
the 38" length of eyelet around the bottom
of the T-shirt. Fold the eyelet pieces down
and press.

2. Lay the T-shirt faceup and flat. Place a
piece of paper inside the T-shirt. Referring
to the photo for placement and using the
disappearing-ink fabric marker and a
variety of bowls and cups, draw 4 circles on
the front of the T-shirt and 1 small circle on
1 sleeve. Beginning at the center of each
circle, draw a swirl that ends at the outer
circle (see the photo). Using the ruler, draw
the lollipop sticks.

3. Remove the paper from inside the T-
shirt. Place the sandpaper inside the T-
shirt, with the rough side facing the front
of the T-shirt. Using the gray paint pen,
paint over the disappearing-ink lines. Let
the paint dry. Referring to the photo and
using the variety of colors of paint pens,
paint each lollipop with fan blade-shaped
sections, being careful not to paint over the
gray lines. Make sure that the sandpaper is
under each lollipop as it is painted. Let the
paint dry. Paint each lollipop with glitter
paint. Let the paint dry.

4. To make each bow, using 1 color of
satin ribbon and leaving a 3" tail, make 3
loops on each side, leaving enough ribbon
to form a second tail. Tack the loops at the
center. Sew or pin 1 ribbon bow to each
lollipop at the top of each stick.

5. Make the boxers, following the
instructions included in the purchased
pattern.

Garden Hats

The prettiest prize of any summer garden is one of these colorful hats, both of which you can make quickly and easily from the same pattern.

You will need (for each hat):
Tracing paper
Pencil
Scissors
Sewing machine
Iron and ironing board
Needle
For the Strawberry Hat: ½ yard red pindot fabric, ¼ yard green pindot fabric, ¼ yard fusible interfacing, white and green thread, ⅝ yard ⅝"-wide green satin ribbon
For the Pea Hat: ¼ yard yellow print fabric, ½ yard green pindot fabric, ¼ yard fusible interfacing, yellow and green thread, ⅝ yard ⅝"-wide green satin ribbon, 6 (¼"-diameter) wooden beads with holes, green acrylic paint, paintbrush, white pipe cleaner

Note: All seams are ¼". You'll find a metric conversion chart on page 5.

1. Using the pencil, transfer the hat panel and leaf patterns on page 125 onto the tracing paper. **For the Strawberry Hat:** Also transfer the strawberry top pattern. Cut out the patterns.

2. For the Strawberry Hat: Transfer the hat panel pattern onto the red pindot 12 times and onto the interfacing 6 times. Cut out the panels. Cut 1 (5" x 44") strip from the green pindot for the brim. Transfer the leaf pattern 4 times and the strawberry top pattern 6 times onto the remaining green pindot. Cut out the leaves and the strawberry tops.

3. Turn the raw edges of the strawberry top pieces under ¼". Press. Referring to the pattern and using the green thread, topstitch 1 strawberry top to 1 red hat panel. Repeat with the remaining strawberry top pieces. Following the manufacturer's instructions, fuse 1 interfacing piece to the back of each stitched hat panel.

4. With the right sides facing and the raw edges aligned, use the white thread to stitch 3 stitched hat panels together. Repeat with the remaining 3 stitched hat panels. Clip the curves and press. With the right sides facing and the raw edges aligned, stitch the panel sets together to make the hat crown. Repeat with the remaining plain hat panel pieces to make the hat crown lining. Set the lining aside.

5. For the stem, cut a 2" x 3½" piece from a green pindot scrap. With the right sides facing and the raw edges aligned, fold the piece in half lengthwise. Using the white thread, stitch along the long raw edges to form a tube. Turn the tube and press. Again, fold the stem in half lengthwise. Topstitch along all of the edges. Set the stem aside.

6. With the right sides facing and the raw edges aligned, use the white thread to stitch 2 leaf pieces together, leaving the bottom edge open. Turn the leaf and press. Repeat with the remaining leaf pieces.

7. Open the seam slightly at the top of the hat crown. Fold the stem in half widthwise and insert ½" of the raw ends into the opening. Fold the leaves so that the seams are in the middle. Insert ½" of the raw end of 1 leaf into the opening on each side of the stem. Restitch the seam closed.

8. With the wrong sides facing and the raw edges aligned, tuck the lining into the hat crown, aligning the seams. Baste along the raw edges. Set the lined hat crown aside.

9. For the hat brim, with the right sides facing and the raw edges aligned, fold the 5" x 44" green pindot strip in half widthwise. Using the white thread, stitch the short ends together to form a ring. Turn. With the wrong sides facing, fold the fabric ring in half lengthwise. Run gathering stitches along the long raw edges. Gather the brim to fit around the lower edge of the hat crown. With the raw edges aligned, stitch the brim to the right side of the lined hat crown. Trim the seam. Fold the hat brim down, with the seam to the inside of the hat. Press. Topstitch the hat close to the brim to keep the brim seam flat.

10. Press the cut ribbon ends under ¼". Pin the ribbon to the inside of the hat, covering the raw edges of the brim. Using the green thread, slipstitch the ribbon in place, being careful to stitch through the lining and the bottom layer of the brim only.

11. **For the Pea Hat:** Transfer the hat panel pattern to the yellow print, the green pindot, and the interfacing 6 times each. Cut out the panels. Cut 1 (5" x 44") strip from the green pindot for the brim. Transfer the leaf pattern to the remaining green pindot 4 times. Cut out the leaves.

12. Following the manufacturer's instructions, fuse 1 interfacing piece to the back of each yellow hat panel. With the right sides facing and the raw edges aligned, use the yellow thread to stitch the yellow hat panels together as in Step 4. Using the green thread, stitch the green hat panels together.

13. Using the green thread, stitch the leaves as in Step 6. Run a gathering stitch around each leaf, ¼" from the edge. Pull the threads to gather. Topstitch the gathers in place. Open the seam slightly at the top of the hat crown. Insert the leaves as in Step 7. Complete steps 8–10.

14. Using the green paint, paint the wooden beads. Let the paint dry. Paint a second coat if desired. Using the green thread, stitch the beads to the middle of the leaves. Center and wrap the pipe cleaner around the base of the leaves. Bend the pipe cleaner ends into curlicues.

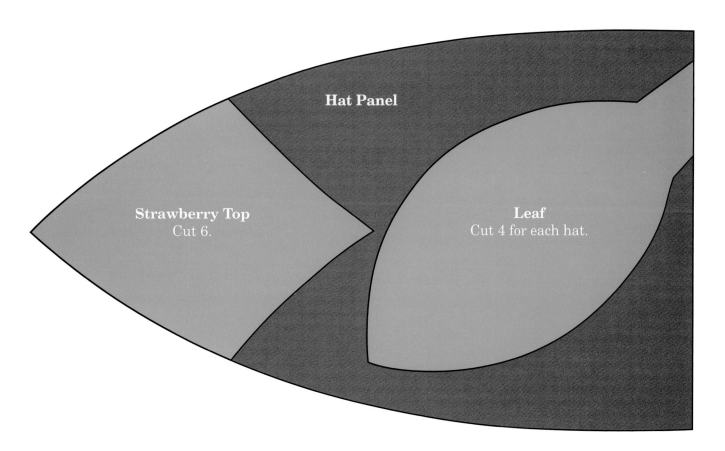

Hat Panel

Strawberry Top
Cut 6.

Leaf
Cut 4 for each hat.

Bug Box and Net

Your mighty adventurer will be king of the anthill when using this critter-catching set to track elusive backyard bugs. And because the bug decorations are made from purchased wooden shapes, they don't require cutting.

You will need (for the box):
Compass
Pieces ¾"-thick wood: 2 (5" x 6"), 1 (5" x 7")
Jigsaw
Electric drill with bits
Acrylic paints: gray-green for base coat,
    variety of colors for bugs
Paintbrushes
2½"-diameter wooden circle
Small brass screw
Screwdriver
Carpenter's wood glue
Carpenter's wood clamps
Variety of small wooden shapes
Thick craft glue
Clear acrylic spray varnish
Wiggle eyes: 6-mm, 3-mm
Fine-tip permanent black marker
8" x 15" piece screen wire
Staple gun and staples
1⅔ yards 1"-wide woven ribbon
Scissors

Note: You'll find a metric conversion chart on page 5.

1. Using the compass, round off the corners on 1 short end of each 5" x 6" wood piece; then mark a 2⅛"-diameter circle on 1 piece, centering the circle 2¾" above the straight edge. Using the jigsaw, cut along the marked corner lines. In the center of the marked circle, drill a hole large enough for the jigsaw blade to pass through. Using the jigsaw, cut out the marked circle.

2. Using the gray-green paint, paint both sides of the rounded wood pieces, the 5" x 7" wood piece, and the 2½"-diameter wooden circle, letting the paint dry on 1 side of each before painting the other side.

3. Center the 2½"-diameter wooden circle over the circle cut in the rounded wood

piece. Screw the brass screw through the top of the wooden circle, making sure the screw goes into the rounded piece behind it. Do *not* tighten the screw completely; leaving the screw slightly loose will allow the "door" to twist open and shut.

4. Apply the wood glue to the short ends of the 5" x 7" wood piece. Butt the straight edge of 1 curved wood piece against each glued end. Hold the pieces in place with the wood clamps until the glue sets.

5. Paint the various wooden shapes as desired to resemble bugs. Let the paint dry. Using the craft glue, glue the bugs onto the sides of the box, making sure the bugs do not interfere with the opening of the door.

Let the glue dry. Spray a coat of the varnish over the entire box. Using the craft glue, glue the wiggle eyes onto the bugs. Let the glue dry. Using the permanent marker, draw legs and antennae for the bugs.

6. Beginning at 1 long side of the bottom piece, wrap the screen over the top of the box to the other side, using the staple gun to secure the screen. From the woven ribbon, cut 1 (10") length, 2 (8½") lengths, and 2 (15") lengths. Staple 1 cut end of the 10" ribbon length to the center top of each curved end to make the handle. Using the craft glue, glue 1 (8½") length to each straight bottom side edge. Glue 1 (15") length to each curved end of the box. Let the glue dry.

You will need (for the net):
36" length ¾"-diameter wooden dowel
Acrylic paints: gray-green for base coat,
    variety of colors for designs
Paintbrushes
Fine-tip permanent black marker
Clear acrylic spray varnish
Wire clothes hanger
Wire cutters
Scissors
1 yard white netting
Sewing machine
White thread
Duct tape
Staple gun and staples
½ yard 1"-wide woven ribbon

1. Paint the dowel gray-green. Let the paint dry. Using a variety of colors, paint bands, dots, and squiggles as desired along the dowel. Let the paint dry. Using the permanent marker, outline the bands. Spray 2 coats of varnish on the dowel, letting the dowel dry between coats.

2. Unwind the clothes hanger. Using the wire cutters, cut off the bent area. Bend the wire into a 9"-diameter circle. Bend each end of the wire into a straight 3" extension.

3. Cut a 36"-diameter circle from the netting. Fold the cut edge under 1". Machine-stitch it in place ½" from the fold, leaving a 2" opening. Insert the wire loop into the casing.

4. Sandwich 1 end of the dowel between the 3" wire extensions. Tightly wrap duct tape around the dowel and the wire extensions. Staple 1 cut end of the ribbon to the top end of the dowel over the duct tape. Wrap the ribbon around the dowel, covering the duct tape. Staple the remaining cut end of the ribbon in place on top of the wrapped ribbon.

Tooth Fairy Doll

When your daughter loses a tooth, slip the tooth into the gingham pocket—she'll be greeted with a surprise in the top pocket the next morning.

You will need:

Tracing paper
Pencil
Scissors
⅛ yard each 45"-wide cotton fabric: green
   gingham, pink gingham
5" x 8" scrap yellow gingham
4" x 5" scrap yellow print
4" x 5" scrap batting
Sewing machine
Thread: white, pink
Stuffing
Craft paints: pink, yellow
Small paintbrushes
Fine-tipped permanent blue fabric marker
Straight pins

Note: All seams are ¼". You'll find a metric conversion chart on page 5.

1. Using the pencil, transfer the patterns to the tracing paper. Cut them out. Transfer the paper patterns and the markings to the fabrics as indicated.

2. With the right sides facing and the raw edges aligned, use the white thread to stitch 2 matching arm pieces together, leaving the top straight edge open. Turn the arm to the right side. Repeat with the remaining arm pieces. Stuff each firmly.

3. Refer to the photo and the patterns to paint the following. On each arm, paint the hand pink. On the body front, paint the face pink and the buttons yellow. On each leg, paint the knee, the heel, and the toe yellow. Let the paint dry. Using the fabric marker, add eyes, a nose, a mouth, and the star-shaped cheeks to the face.

4. For each sleeve, turn the bottom edge under ⅛" twice. Machine-baste the hem in place, leaving long threads at the beginning and the end of the stitching. With the right

sides facing and the raw edges aligned, stitch the underarm sleeve seam, keeping the basting threads free; press. Turn the sleeve to the right side. Insert 1 arm into the sleeve. Pull up the bobbin thread until the hemmed edge of the sleeve fits snugly around the lower portion of the arm. Knot the thread ends together.

5. To make the skirt, fold the waist edge under ⅛" twice. Using the white thread, topstitch. Fold the small pocket in half, with the wrong sides together. Referring to the placement lines on the skirt pattern and using the pink thread, satin-stitch the small pocket in place on the right side of the skirt. With the right sides faceup and the raw edges aligned, pin the skirt to the body front.

6. With the right sides together and the raw edges aligned, stitch 2 matching leg pieces together, leaving the top straight edge open. Repeat with the remaining leg pieces. Turn them to the right side. Stuff each firmly.

7. With the front of the legs facing the right side of the skirt/body and the raw edges aligned, center and baste the legs on the bottom edge of the skirt/body. With the front of each sleeve/arm facing the right side of the body and the raw edges aligned, baste 1 sleeve/arm to each side of the body.

8. With the right sides facing, the raw edges aligned, and the arms and the legs toward the center, stitch the body front and back together, catching the skirt in the seam and leaving the bottom edge of the body open. Turn the body to the right side. Stuff the body firmly. Slipstitch the opening closed.

9. To make the hair, from a pink gingham scrap, cut 1 (2"-diameter) circle. Fold the circle in half. Make cuts around the edge toward the center of the circle. Place the circle on the back of the head so that the fabric hair surrounds the face. Handstitch the hair in place. Trim to make bangs if desired.

10. To make the wings, with the right sides facing and the raw edges aligned, stack the yellow gingham wing pieces. Place the batting wing piece on top. Stitch the layers together ¼" from the raw edge, leaving an opening for turning. Clip small notches in the seam allowance. Turn the wings right side out. Slipstitch the opening closed. Baste along the center line. Pull the threads to gather slightly. Handstitch the wings to the center back of the body.

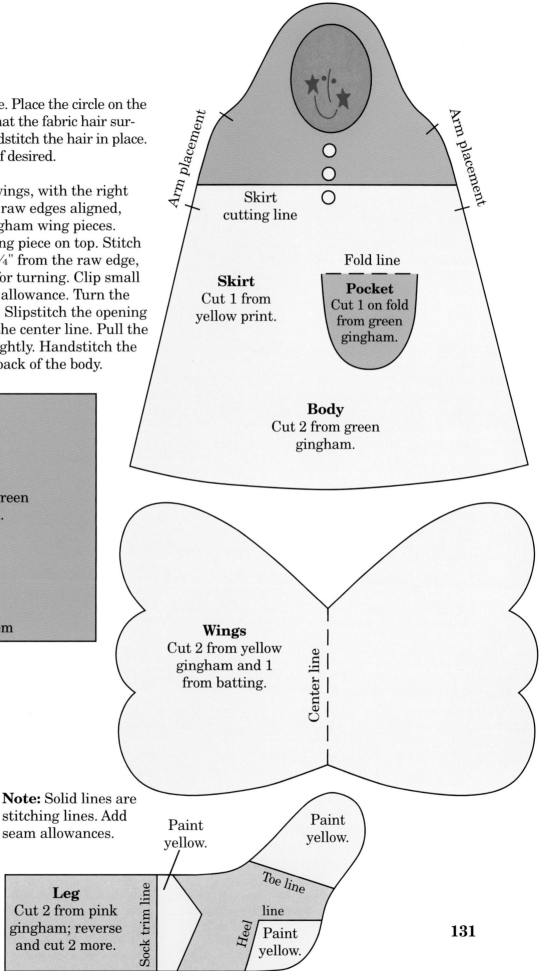

Sleeve
Cut 2 from green gingham.

Rolled hem

Leave open.

Arm
Cut 4 from pink gingham.

Paint pink.

Note: Solid lines are stitching lines. Add seam allowances.

Arm placement

Arm placement

Skirt cutting line

Fold line

Skirt
Cut 1 from yellow print.

Pocket
Cut 1 on fold from green gingham.

Body
Cut 2 from green gingham.

Wings
Cut 2 from yellow gingham and 1 from batting.

Center line

Paint yellow.

Paint yellow.

Toe line

line

Heel

Paint yellow.

Sock trim line

Leg
Cut 2 from pink gingham; reverse and cut 2 more.

131

Lily Pad Larry

When lovable Larry lands in his lap, your child will know he has just met a special friend. His mouth and legs are movable, which makes him all the more playful.

You will need:
Tracing paper
Pencil
Yardstick
Scissors
Disappearing-ink fabric marker
⅝ yard 60"-wide green polar fleece
Felt scraps: red, pink
Thread: green, red, pink
Needle
Stuffing
Sewing machine
Straight pins
Fabric glue
2 (40-mm) wiggle eyes

Note: All seams are ¼". You'll find a metric conversion chart on page 5.

1. To make the frog body pattern, draw an 11¼"-diameter circle on the tracing paper. Draw a 5¼"-diameter circle above the 11¼"-diameter circle so that the edges touch. Using the yardstick, draw lines connecting the circles as shown. Add ¼" seam allowance. Cut out the pattern. Separately transfer each of the green, red, and pink mouth patterns on page 135 onto the tracing paper, adding ¼" seam allowance to each piece. Transfer the leg patterns on pages 135—137 and the markings to the tracing paper, adding ¼" seam allowance to each. Cut out the individual mouth patterns and the leg patterns.

2. To mark the body pattern, measure straight down 4½" from the top edge of the smaller circle. Draw a line across the pattern at this point. Mark an X on each edge where the line intersects. These are the placement marks for the top edge of the front legs. Locate the center bottom edge of the large circle. Along the seam line, measure 2" to the right from this center point

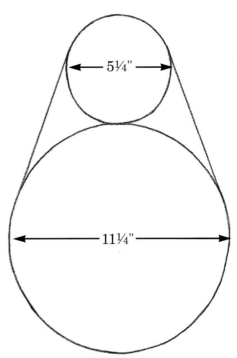

Body Pattern Diagram

and mark with an X. Repeat, measuring and marking 2" to the left of the center bottom point. These are the placement marks for the bottom edge of the hind legs.

3. Using the disappearing-ink fabric marker, transfer the patterns and the markings to the fabric. From the green polar fleece, cut 2 body pieces and 4 each of the front and hind legs; with the green mouth pattern placed on the fold, cut 1. From the red felt, cut 1 red mouth piece. From the pink felt, cut 1 pink mouth piece.

4. To make the eyes, cut 2 (4½"-diameter) circles from the remaining green polar fleece. Using the green thread, run gathering stitches as close to the edge of each circle as possible. Pull the threads to gather slightly. Stuff the eyes. Then pull the threads tightly; tack to secure. Set the eyes aside.

5. With the right sides facing, using the green thread and leaving the straight edge open, machine stitch 2 front leg pieces together. Repeat with the remaining front leg pieces. Repeat for the hind legs. Turn the legs right side out and stuff firmly.

133

6. Lay the green mouth piece flat. Referring to the mouth pattern for placement, pin the red mouth piece in place at 1 end. Using the red thread, stitch the red mouth piece in place. Position the pink mouth piece on top of the red mouth piece. Pin a small pleat along the back straight edge of the pink mouth piece. Using the pink thread, stitch the pink mouth piece in place, leaving the back straight edge open. Insert a little stuffing into the pink mouth piece; stitch the back open edge closed.

7. With the green mouth piece unfolded and the right sides facing, align the plain end of the mouth piece with the narrow end of 1 body piece. Using green thread, stitch from the fold line at 1 edge to the opposite fold line as shown. Fold the stitched half of the mouth under and the tongue half of the mouth up so that the right side of the tongue section of the mouth is faceup. With the right sides facing, pin the remaining body piece to the tongue half of the mouth, as shown. Stitch as before.

8. With the legs toward the center and the raw edges aligned, pin the legs in place, with the top edge of the front legs at the 4½" mark and the bottom edge of the hind legs at the lower leg markings on the body as shown. Beginning at the mouth, stitch around the frog body through all of the thicknesses, leaving the area between the hind legs open. Turn the frog right side out.

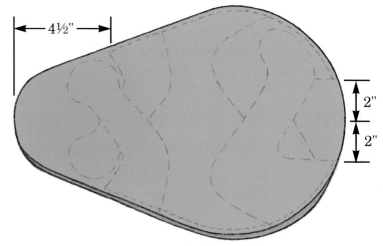

9. Open the mouth. Stitch across the lower half of the mouth along the fold line.

10. Stuff the frog body firmly. Slipstitch the opening closed.

11. Referring to the photo, place the fabric eyes on top of the head area so that the circles touch. Sew them in place. Glue the wiggle eyes toward the front of the fabric eyes. Let the glue dry.

12. To define the toes, thread the needle with doubled green thread. Knot the ends of the thread together. Push the needle up through the bottom of the foot area at 1 marked dot. Loop the thread around the end of the foot and then push the needle up through the bottom of the foot again at the same point. Repeat several times. Pull the thread tightly and tie off. Repeat at each marked dot.

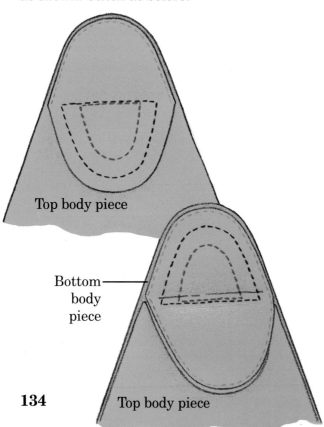

Top body piece

Bottom body piece

Top body piece

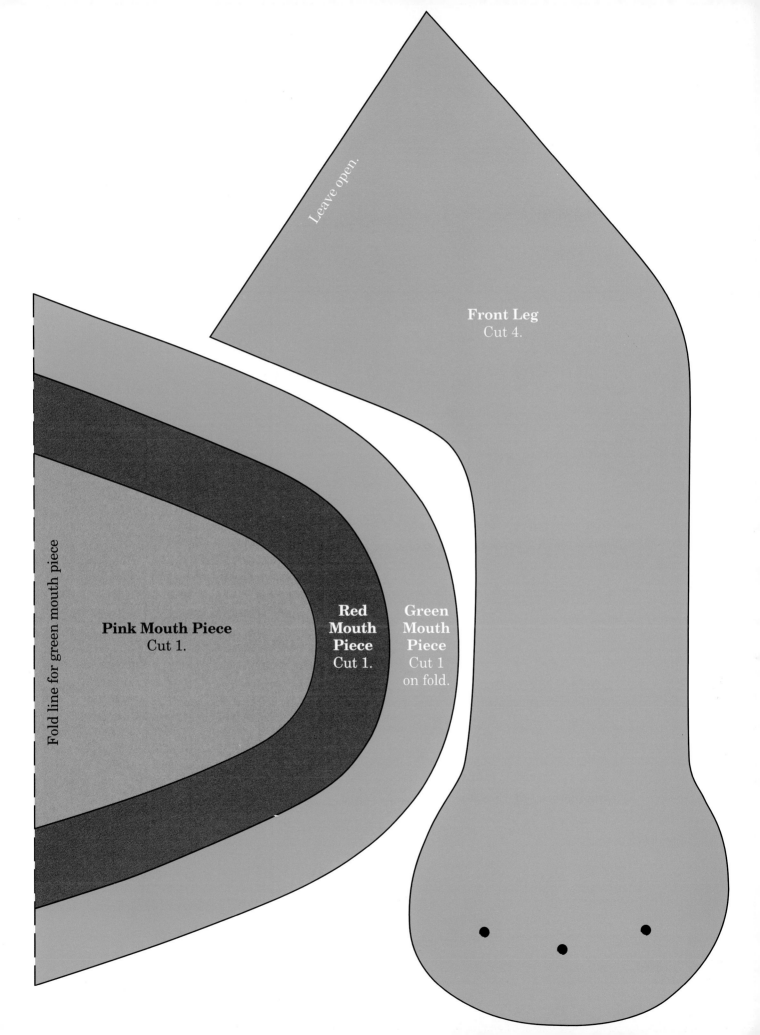

Leave open.

Front Leg
Cut 4.

Fold line for green mouth piece

Pink Mouth Piece
Cut 1.

Red Mouth Piece
Cut 1.

Green Mouth Piece
Cut 1 on fold.

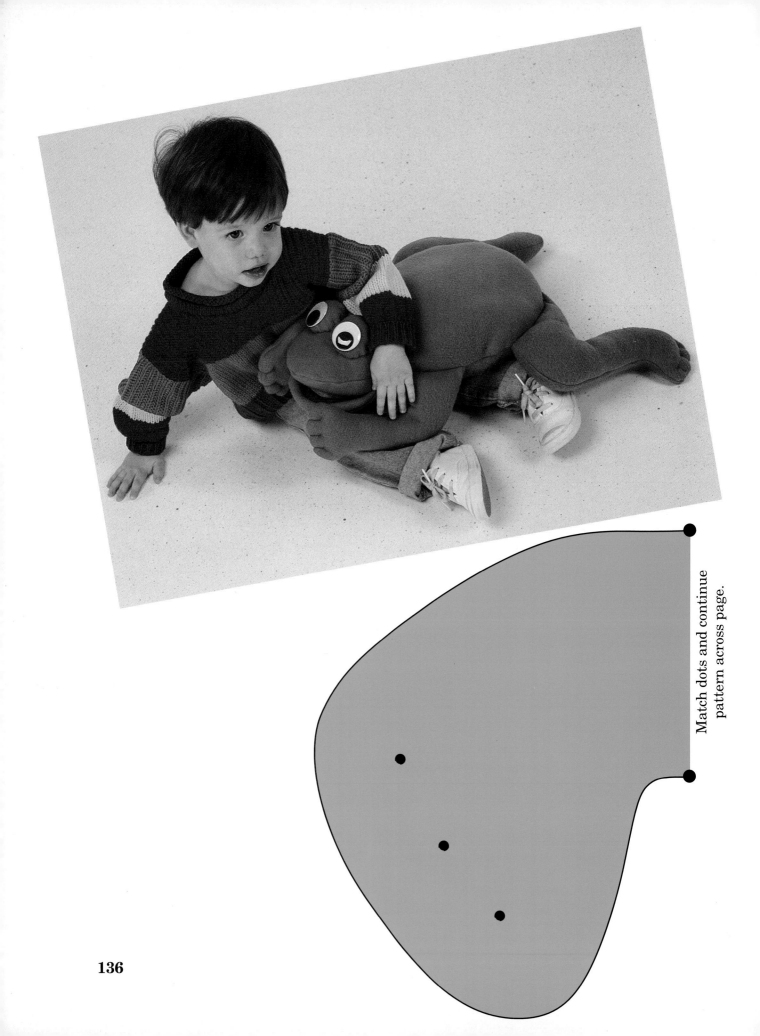

Match dots and continue pattern across page.

Hind Leg
Cut 4.

Soccer Satchel

This duffle is on the ball! It's just the right size to hold a team uniform, a pair of cleats, and a water bottle.

You will need:

Canvas fabric: ⅝ yard black, ¼ yard white
Tape measure
Scissors
Pencil
¼ yard paper-backed fusible web
Iron and ironing board
Thread: black, white
Sewing machine
Candle
Match
2¼ yards 1"-wide black nylon belting
2⅝ yards ⅜"-wide white grosgrain ribbon
18" black nylon zipper
Straight pins

Note: You'll find a metric conversion chart on page 5.

1. From the black canvas, cut 2 (18" x 20¾") pieces. From the white canvas, cut 4 (9") squares.

2. Using the pencil, trace 2 of each black soccer ball patch shape on page 140 onto the paper side of the fusible web. (For a total of 12 patches.) Following the manufacturer's instructions, fuse the traced patches to the wrong side of a black canvas scrap. Cut out the shapes. Divide the patches into 2 stacks, placing 1 of each patch shape in each stack.

3. Place 1 white canvas square faceup on the soccer ball pattern. Using the pencil, transfer the outer circle to the center of the square. Leave the square positioned on top of the pattern. Remove the paper backing from 1 stack of patches and pin the patches in place. Remove the square and following the manufacturer's instructions, fuse the patches in place, removing pins as you work. Replace the square on top of the pattern and, using the pencil, trace the soccer ball lines.

4. Using the black thread, satin-stitch along the edges of the black patches and along the traced lines. With the wrong sides facing, stack the soccer ball square on top of a plain white canvas square. Stitch the squares together along the inside of the soccer ball outline. Trim the soccer ball along the drawn outline. Repeat steps 3 and 4 with the remaining white canvas squares. These soccer balls are the end pieces of the bag.

5. To prevent the cut ends of the nylon belting from raveling, carefully run the ends through a candle or match flame. Center the white ribbon along the length of the nylon belting. Trim the excess ribbon. Turn each end of the belting under 1". Using the white thread in the top of the sewing machine and the black thread in the bobbin, stitch the ribbon in place.

6. To make the bag, with the wrong sides facing, stack the 2 (18" x 20¾") black canvas pieces. Using the black thread and a medium-width zigzag, stitch around all edges. With the belting strap faceup, position the strap on the black canvas as shown.

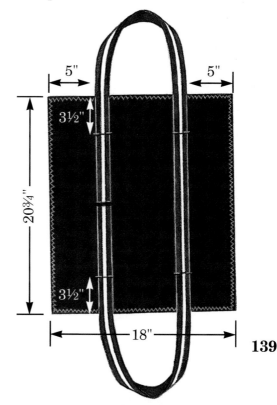

7. With the zipper facedown on the right side of the fabric, align 1 edge of the zipper tape with 1 (18") edge of the black canvas. Stitch ¼" from the edge. Press the canvas away from the zipper. Topstitch. Repeat along the remaining 18" edge of the canvas with the remaining edge of the zipper tape.

8. With the right sides facing, pin 1 soccer ball end piece to 1 end of the bag. Stitch ¼" from the edge. Unzip the bag approximately 4". Pin the remaining soccer ball piece to the opposite end of the bag. Stitch in place. Zigzag to clean-finish all the seams. Turn the bag right side out.

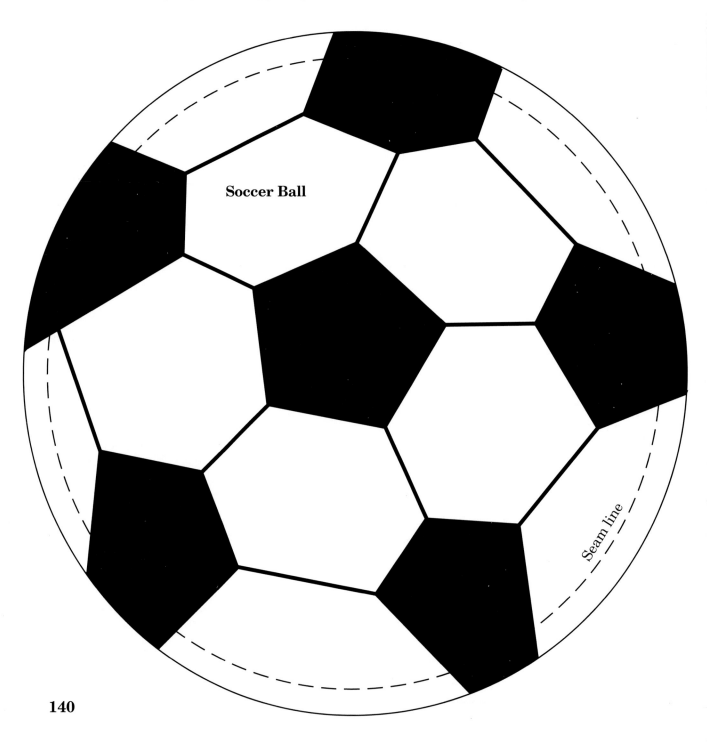

Soccer Ball

Seam line

Blue Jeans Pocket Purse

A worn-out pair of jeans finds new life as a stylish purse for some lucky young miss.

You will need:

7" pink zipper
Denim: 2 (9½") squares, 1 pocket, 2" x 36" strip for strap
Sewing machine
Thread: blue, tan
Iron and ironing board
12 purchased fabric yo-yos for decorating purse
½ yard ⅜"-wide pink ruffled grosgrain ribbon
Buttons: 15 various novelty and regular, 2 matching for strap
3 sew-on charms
Needle
Ruler
Pencil
Scissors
1 yard ⅝"-wide pink grosgrain ribbon
¼ yard ¼"-wide pink satin ribbon

Note: To make your own yo-yos, cut 2¼"-diameter circles from the fabrics of your choice. Turn under ¼" along the edge of each circle. Run gathering stitches around the edge of each circle, stitching through both layers. Pull the thread tightly, gathering the edge to the center. Knot the thread to secure. Tack at the center to hold the fabric in place. You'll find a metric conversion chart on page 5.

1. With the side edge aligned, center the zipper facedown on the right side of 1 edge of 1 denim square. (The denim should extend ½" on each end of the zipper tape.) Machine-stitch, using the blue thread and a ¼" seam. Center and stitch the remaining side of the zipper to the right side of 1 edge of the remaining denim square in the same manner. Press the seams away from the zipper and topstitch the denim on each side of the zipper.

2. Center and pin the pocket faceup on the right side of 1 denim square, with the top edge of the pocket 1" below the zipper. Using the tan thread and stitching along the side and bottom edges, machine-stitch the pocket in place on the denim square. Referring to the photo, position the yo-yos, the ruffled ribbon, the buttons, and the charms as desired. Using the blue thread, handstitch the decorations on the pocket in place, being careful to stitch through the pocket layer only. Handstitch the remaining decorations in place on the denim square.

3. Open the zipper 2". With the right sides facing and the raw edges aligned, machine-stitch the 2 denim squares together along the side and bottom edges, using the blue thread and a ½" seam.

4. To square off each top corner of the purse, align the zipper teeth with 1 side seam. Measure and mark ¾" along each edge from the point. Machine-stitch straight across from mark to mark as shown.

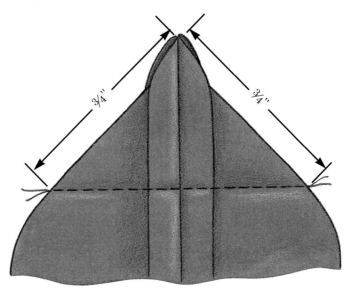

Trim the corner, leaving a ¼" seam allowance. Repeat for the bottom corners, aligning the bottom seam of the purse with the side seams. Turn the purse right side out.

5. To shape the edges of the bag, flatten 1 side seam. Using the blue thread, topstitch along 1 edge close to the edge of the fabric as shown. Repeat for the remaining edge. Repeat for the remaining side seam and the bottom seam.

6. To make the strap, with the wrong sides together, fold the long edges of the strip to the middle. Press. Center the ⅝"-wide ribbon along the length of the strip, covering the raw edges. Using the blue thread, straightstitch along both long edges of the ribbon. Turn each end of the strap under 1". Stitch to secure. Position 1 end of the strap faceup on 1 side of the purse, with the folded end of the strap 1½" below the zipper. Stitch the strap in place. Repeat to attach the remaining end to the remaining side. Handstitch 1 button to each side of the strap to cover the stitching.

7. To make the zipper pull, fold the ¼"-wide ribbon in half. Insert the folded end through the hole in the zipper tab to make a loop. Slip the cut ends of the ribbon through the loop and pull until the ribbon is snug against the zipper tab. Trim the ends of the ribbon at an angle.

Designers & Contributors

Jennifer Alleavitch, Teatime Pin, 80; Reindeer Tie, 112

James P. Barnhart, Bug Box (concept), 126

Amy Albert Bloom, Critter Ornaments, 21; Critter Cloth, 25

Marilyn M. Carlton, Paint Stick Ornaments, 74

Phyllis Dunstan, Reindeer Sweatshirts, 12; Wire Stars, 51

Debby Gaston, Fancy Gloves and Headbands, 118

Linda Hendrickson, Tooth Fairy Doll (concept), 129

Heidi Tyline King, Five Golden Rings, 10; Jingle Bell Bracelets, 16; Measuring Tree, 63; Pom-pom Gift Tags, 71; Ring in the Holidays, 72; Garden Hats, 122

Françoise Dudal Kirkman, Layered Felt Stocking, 30; Tissue Paper Candles, 78; Sea Sculptures, 96

Connie Matricardi, North Pole Finger Puppets, 67

Barbara McNorton Neel, Antlered Greetings, 18; Glowing Globes, 44; Cutwork Pillowcases, 92

Susan G. Peele, Fantastic Frames, 84; Permanent Prints, 91

Betsy Cooper Scott, Flashlight Torch, 8; Desk Set, 103; Funky Flowers for Your Feet, 105; Angel Sweatshirt, 115; Sweet Dreams Sleepwear, 120; Lily Pad Larry, 132

Joan M. Sleeth, Glittery Snowflakes, 46

Elizabeth Taliaferro, Gold Medal Door Decoration, 37; Concession Stand, 40

Karen T. Tillery, Wintertime Waders, 48; Holly Jolly Gift Wrap, 57; Seeing Stars, 60; Collectible Keepers, 108

Carol Tipton, Ribbon Wand, 36; Garland Relay, 38; Bug Box and Net, 126; Tooth Fairy Doll, 129

Cynthia Moody Wheeler, Gold Leaf Table Runner, 54; Botanical Bookmarks, 88; Soccer Satchel, 138; Blue Jeans Pocket Purse, 141

Alexa M. Whitehead, Botanical Bookmarks (concept), 88

Special thanks to the following shops in Birmingham, Alabama, for sharing their resources with *Christmas is Coming:* **Jack N' Jill Shop; Sikes Children's Shoes.**